A Willful Child

A Willful Child

JANET STEELE HOLLOWAY

authorHOUSE®

AuthorHouse™
1663 Liberty Drive
Bloomington, IN 47403
www.authorhouse.com
Phone: 1-800-839-8640

Published by AuthorHouse   10/17/2012

ISBN: 978-1-4772-8108-6 (sc)
ISBN: 978-1-4772-8107-9 (hc)
ISBN: 978-1-4772-8106-2 (e)

Library of Congress Control Number: 2012919471

Excerpt

"My father and his friend George usually started drinking in the kitchen while my mother and Betty would get "made up" for their Friday evening. My mother perched in front of the maple dresser, pulling on her nylon stockings, carefully adjusting the seams, blotting the blue-red lipstick on toilet paper, tucking stray ends of auburn hair with black hair pins. Laughing and gossiping, she took her time deciding what jewelry to wear, holding up various earrings, turning her head this way and that, while Betty, using the Maybelline brush, gave careful attention to her dark eyebrows. I'd lie on the bed watching them and listening to their stories and the clinking of ice in their glasses; the combined smell of Seagrams 7, Tabu perfume and cigarette smoke filling my imagination about what it meant to be a grown-up woman."

Janet Holloway is not afraid to show the broken side of her life. She excels at pulling you in and pulling on your heart strings and you don't ever want the stories to end. She captures place and dialogue and action with all her senses—an outstanding and profound story teller!

Martha Layne Collins, Former Governor, Commonwealth of Kentucky

Acknowledgements

I've been an off-and-on writer all my life. As a child I wrote poems, songs and stories; kept a diary; scribbled in journals and on scraps of paper, and had dreams of being a famous author someday. That was then.

For the past several years, I've been a reporter and a contributor to newspapers and magazines, always focused on telling others' stories: where they've come from, what they've done, what they've learned. It takes time to tell one's own story, to get as close to the truth as you can. It has to be revealed, almost relived, before discovering a kernel of truth.

A Willful Child is my attempt to write that story, an account of my formative years. The stories tell of betrayals, secrets and new beginnings. Some names have been changed* to protect innocent souls. The stories may not reflect exactly what happened, but they are the way I remember them.

I would never have written this book without the encouragement and support of my friends at the Carnegie Center for Literacy and Learning in Lexington, Kentucky. Thanks to Neil Chethik and Jan Isenhour for always telling me to "just keep writing," when I tried to make sense out of what I was producing. There's a special place in my heart for Leatha Kendrick, my teacher, my friend and editor, who pushed and pulled and dared me to "go deeper" each time I showed her rough drafts. Flo Brumley, Alexander Hume, Pam Holman and Sam Stephens inspired and encouraged me from the beginning.

Thanks to Mindy Shannon Phelps for her copy edits, Helene Steene and Luisa Trujillo for their artistry and design. A special thank you to all my friends who took me seriously as a writer, long before I could, and to my brother Dan and sister-in-law Linda Steele, cousins Donald and Ellen Branscome for their encouragement and remembrance of things past.

Dedicated to
Adele Kaplan, my dearest friend for more than 30 years
&
John Patrick O'Connor, who has loved me
through it all, thick and thin

In memory of
Rebecca "Billie" Spriggs Brownie Gartin, my grandmother
Melba Brownie Steele Schroll, my mother
Millard F. Steele, Jr., my father

©

Janet Steele Holloway

Contents

Epilogue

The Möbius strip has several curious properties. A line drawn starting from the seam down the middle will meet back at the seam but at the "other side." If continued the line will meet the starting point and will be double the length of the original strip. This single continuous curve demonstrates that the Möbius strip has only one boundary. Where the line ends is where it starts again. Beginning and end are fused and overlapping.

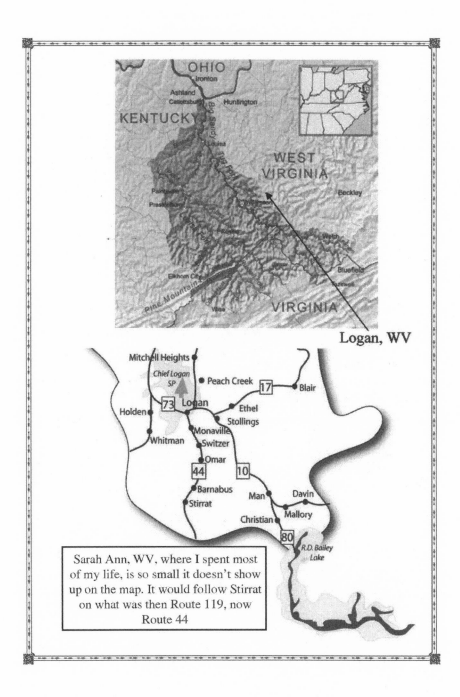

Logan, WV

Sarah Ann, WV, where I spent most of my life, is so small it doesn't show up on the map. It would follow Stirrat on what was then Route 119, now Route 44

*Picture a wild green density cut by cramped, intimate hollers
tucked into steep hillsides and . . . winding, dizzying roads that
seem . . . tentative, as if always threatening to break off on
the edges or collapse and fall to ruins among the forests, and
weeds . . . . Imagine a world that dwells in the space of the gap,
in a logic of negation, surprise, contingency, roadblock, and
perpetual incompletion.*

A Space Beside of the Road, Kathleen Stewart

A Willful Child

1944, Switzer (Logan County), West Virginia

It was a burning summer in the West Virginia mountains in 1944, with humidity settling down heavily on everything that moved.

I wanted an ice cream so badly I tortured my mother with down-on-the-floor, screaming tantrums until she opened the front door and screamed back, "Well, go get it then."

I was three years old. We were living in Switzer, in a small white house just off Route 119, the main road that led to the county seat. It was the first of dozens of places we would live in over the next sixteen years.

"Go get it," she said again, pointing to the quarter-mile curve where Johnson's Grocery claimed the only retail site in Switzer. "Just stay off that highway. Stay on the dirt side, Miss Priss."

I can imagine my pouty, chubby face; feel the sweat on my head and the determination in my spine to get what I wanted.

I walked off the porch, looking at the distant store, turning back to look home only once. Mother stood on the front porch, my baby brother on her hip, flailing about, fighting sleep.

Few cars passed on the road and when they did, the yellowish dirt from the shoulders rose like mist and resettled on patches of wild grass and thicket on the creek side. The blacktop shimmered with heat. The hot summer day let loose a dense crop of grasshoppers, and their smell reminded me of the fireflies we'd chase on summer evenings. Grasshoppers flying among the weeds didn't come close to distracting me from my goal, but Johnson's Grocery seemed awfully far away.

I kept to the side of the road, like Mother told me, kicking rocks, scuffing my shoes. The neighbors' yards were quiet, empty of children and dogs. I could hear the hum of electric fans in front of open windows. It seemed no one wanted to be out in the mid-day sun.

As I neared Johnson's, I saw an old man sweeping the dirt in front of the store. He stopped, took off his cap, and nodded as I opened the screen door and went in. The ceiling fan moved around the hot air in the store, where Andy Johnson was draped across the meat cooler, smoking a cigarette. No one else was inside.

Stella, Andy's wife and my Granny Bill's sister, came from behind the curtain that led to a storage room after she heard the bell on the screen door.

"Why, 'pon my honor! Look who's here," Stella called out. "Where's your momma? Melba's not with you?"

Stella favored my granny in looks but there was something about her that seemed scary and witchlike.

The Johnsons seemed pleased to see me. Andy tried to pick me up but I pulled away, staying close to the check-out counter, out of his reach. His lower lip was always wet and nasty looking, and I couldn't stop staring at it.

Stella kept saying, as she wiped the counter, "Where's your momma, little girl?" I told her she was at home. Stella looked at Andy and frowned.

Andy Johnson gave me the frozen Creamsicle I wanted and asked if I'd like to sign the bill. I shook my head no and he laughed, his extended belly bouncing as he did. Stella picked up the phone and gave the operator a number to call, waving her handkerchief at me as I pushed open the screen door.

"Don't you want to sit a spell, cool off?" she called out, moving her ample frame to a high stool behind the counter.

"No, thank you."

I headed for home.

On the way back, I thought of nothing but the ice cream in my hand. Then, for some reason, I stopped. I stopped and looked at the highway. I was tempted, but why? Because it was there? Because I was free, for that moment, of my mother's requirements? Because I was angry with her?

I looked to the left and I looked to the right, just like I'd been taught. I put one foot on the black top, then pulled it back, very, very slowly.

I re-focused on my melting ice cream and getting home.

There she was, sitting on the steps. "You better watch your ass, little girl," Mother growled as she stood and held open the screen door.

I said nothing but headed for the bathroom to wash the stickiness from my hands.

"You just always have to be one step over that line, don't you?" she followed. "You better start paying me some mind, girl, or you're going to be sorry."

I went into the room I shared with my two-year-old brother. He was sound asleep, and I curled up on the rug beside his crib, listening to him breathe.

I heard the phone ring and could tell it was Granny Bill because of the way my mom was talking. I heard the sharp edge in her voice as she said, "Stella had no right to be calling you. Nobody knows what a handful this child can be!"

I must have fallen asleep because the next thing I remember was the sound of Granny's voice in our living room, telling my mother to keep her voice down.

"Melba, you don't know what you're saying." Granny spoke in a loud whisper. "There's no way you're leaving here."

"I can't stand it anymore," I heard my mother say. "My head feels like it's going to blow off. I can't do anything right. He never helps out. He comes home from the mines and goes to that couch and sleeps 'til dinner."

My mother's voice was high and breathless.

"He's worked hard all day, honey," Granny said. "He's entitled to some rest."

"What about me? When am I entitled to something? I feel like I'm going crazy and nobody's doing anything about it. Nobody cares what's happening to me."

I heard the screen door slam, and I scrambled off the floor. Danny was still asleep. In the living room, Granny stood near the electric fan, holding out her skirt to catch the cool air.

Seeing me, she said, "She'll be back, honey. Don't you worry. She'll be back."

My mother liked for Danny and me to look good, present a "good face" as she called it. Not true for Granny Bill: she didn't care what we wore as long as we had clothes on. These photos show me at 4 and 5, with my brother, a year younger.

What's In a Name?

1946, Omar, West Virginia

Family rumors about my mother's birth and legitimacy rose up or faded away depending on the state of Granny Bill's health over the years. Granny always countered any query about Mother's birth with, "It's none of your damned business. She's my baby!"

When a doctor diagnosed Granny with her first cancer, the rumor mill cranked into high gear, with her siblings fearing my mother would inherit what they felt was rightfully theirs. It wasn't that Granny had so much money; it was just that, with her various businesses—some legal, some not—she had more than anybody else in her family and they all wanted it.

My mother's interest in her origins wasn't strange at all; it fit with her lifetime insecurity and feeling that she never belonged anywhere. Even as a child, she told me, she never felt part of Granny's extended family.

To start with, her name, Melba, was an unusual one; no one else we knew had a name like it. Mom always said she was named after Nellie Melba, an Australian opera singer in the early 1920's. Mom sometimes produced an old newspaper photo and article from her *Book of Dreams*. The tattered, yellowing photograph showed Nellie Melba lounging in a plush, overstuffed chair, smiling seductively at the camera, all the while buttoned up from her chin to her boots.

The article highlighted her career.

"Nellie Melba had . . . abandoned her family in Melbourne for her career and . . . according to her contemporary [and rival], Emma Eames ' . . . if a singer's greatness can be gauged by how detested she was by colleagues, then Melba would undoubtedly be the greatest singer of all time.'"

The article went on to describe how Melba tolerated no rivals; tenor John McCormack, on the night of his London debut, apparently attempted to take a bow with her on stage. She pushed him back forcefully and reportedly said, "In this house, no one takes a bow with Melba!"

What I remember most from that article, lodged in the *"Dreams of Being Chased"* section of Mom's *Dream Book*, was the expression, "more comebacks than Nellie Melba," satirizing Melba's endless series of retirement tours in the 1920's.

I smiled at the similarity of both women. My mother had made quite a few comebacks herself.

What was agreed upon among family members was that my mother was born on August 8, 1922, outside of Abingdon, Virginia. Whether she actually was put in a basket and left on Granny's doorstep, as some said, or given to her by a friend of the birth mother, has never been verified by anyone. Both stories were passed

8

around the family, and, because I was only four or five at the time, the adults talked about it in front of me, thinking I was too young to understand anything.

My own research into courthouse documents years later revealed only that Granny Bill—Rebecca "Billie" Spriggs—had married Chester Brownie in 1920. They had one child, Arthur, who died within a few months. That's all that can be confirmed. And then a year or so after Arthur died, my mother was brought into their lives.

From what I gathered, Chester didn't stay around very long after that. The family story was that Chester went out for razorblades one night and never came back.

The Early Days

1935, Logan County, West Virginia

Uncle Paul was my mother's first boyfriend, when she was thirteen, in 1935.

"He smelled like lilac soap," she told me. "He had the prettiest curly brown hair and big blue eyes," she told me. "I had such a crush on him."

My heart must have fluttered with the thought that she, too, once had a crush on my favorite uncle.

I was around five or six when she told me this story of Uncle Paul and how he introduced her to my dad for the first time. I was excited, expecting a fairy tale, filled with romance and happy endings.

"There was an event in the auditorium of the Omar Grade and Junior High School where students were performing," she said, "and I sang *The Beautiful Lady in Blue,* wearing my new, blue dress."

I smiled at my beautiful, lip-sticked mother, imagining her on stage. She sang around the house when she was happy—songs like *Allegheny Moon* and *Red Sails in the Sunset*—and it made me happy to hear her sing. Her voice was throaty and deep, she said, because of all the cigarettes she smoked.

Wide eyed, I waited for her to continue, impatient to hear how she and daddy fell in love.

"Paul was so much better looking than your father, and fun to be with."

This wasn't exactly the fairy tale I was expecting. I wondered if I'd heard her right.

"Paul came backstage with Millard, your dad, who shook my hand and said, 'I'm happy to meet the beautiful girl in blue in person.'"

I held my breath. Maybe it will have a happy ending after all.

"I liked Paul better; he liked to laugh and tease me. He had a reputation for being a little wild, even though he came from a good family. Your dad was older, more serious. But once your Granny Bill met Millard, that was it. She wouldn't let me date anyone else. I was thirteen."

She made it sound like Granny was bad for doing this. My granny? There had to be more.

"So what happened then?" My eyes stared, my mouth hung open, wanting a happy ending and afraid I wouldn't get one.

"So your dad and I got married on my sixteenth birthday and you were born two years later."

A sensible close, on the surface, but something didn't feel right. My stomach growled, like I was hungry or getting sick. Her story confused me. Who was I supposed to root for in this story?

Who was the prince? Where was Cinderella? In this fairy tale, it seemed like everybody lost something, though I couldn't explain what.

As a child, I followed my Uncle Paul everywhere. I snuggled into his lap on Granny Steele's front porch swing after he had washed off the coal dust. I sat on the toilet seat to watch him shave, fought with my brother to get the seat next to him in the car. As much as I loved my father, I adored my Uncle Paul—his easy laughs and chuckles, the teasing, the way he always made me feel like I was his girl, sitting on his lap in the swing, singing, counting the coal cars passing through downtown Logan. He once told me that the more coal cars we could count, the happier everyone would be. I tried hard to learn my numbers after that.

I was born in Uncle Paul's room on Flag Day, 1941. Some said that my dad's mom—Granny Steele—and one of my aunts pulled me out, and Dr. Carney arrived just in time to cut the cord and give my mom a sleeping pill. Others, including my mother, denied it and made it clear that Dr. Carney did the job.

Years later, I tried to remember if Uncle Paul had ever married. Mother's reply was terse.

"Paul never did get married, although he dated some Hunky girl for a few years before he died. You know he died in the mines? He was on his back digging coal when he smelled gas. He raised up real fast and hit his head on one of those support beams and it killed him."

Why did she keep reminding me of this? I was ten when he died and had heard the story dozens of times. It always made me sad. She knew it made me sad, so why remind me of it?

Granny Steele's tiny cinderblock house in downtown Logan, West Virginia, backed up to a cemetery on a narrow street that overlooked the Guyandotte River and the railroad tracks. As kids, when we visited Granny Steele and our aunts and uncles, we used the cemetery as our playground, playing hide and seek in the hollow vaults and empty statues.

Many a night I'd awaken to the sound of the train whistle; I'd climb out of the bed I shared with my Aunt Shirley at the time and curl up at the foot of Uncle Paul's bed, thrilled with the sound of the train and Paul's soft snore.

What was it that bound me to him as a child? Did my body infuse the fragrance of his Old Spice and Brilliantine into my molecular structure? Did the static of his short-wave radio configure the synapses of my young brain? Could it be that the evening train whistle laid the tracks for my passion to travel, to move on, move out? Perhaps it was simply the fact that I was given his name, Janet Paul. Mother used to wonder aloud about my attachment to Paul.

I had no questions about it. It just was.

Sixteen. Mother married my dad at sixteen, when he was nineteen, in 1938. She'd just finished tenth grade, and he'd graduated high school with honors and worked for Mason White, installing records on juke boxes in restaurants and beer gardens around Logan County. They eloped on her sixteenth birthday, driving to Canada, Kentucky, where no signature was required.

I often wonder if that impulsiveness was a symptom of her later illness. It certainly characterized her later years, like the time, in the winter when I was eleven, I came home from school to find the note on the mantle. I didn't cry, like my brother and father did. Somehow, I knew I had to be strong. I emptied a can of green beans into a pot and turned on the stove, like my dad told me, then took a bath while they cooked, splashing the tepid water in the pink bathtub with my legs, shaking my head fast, whispering, "I won't cry. I won't cry." Trying to erase the words, "I'm sorry to leave you all. I have to go away."

That departure and loss were to be repeated over the years.

I don't have many memories of my father before he came home from World War II in 1946, when I was five. There are pictures of me at about twelve months, just beginning to walk. I'm smiling, held up on his shoulder. He's looking dapper in his dress khakis and perfectly pressed shirt, sometimes holding a cigarette. He left for basic training in Texas in 1944 and then for Japan when I was about three or four. He spent a year, year and a half in Okinawa during the Occupation.

The war required sacrifices of everyone. Even as children, we were encouraged to save the silver covering from any chewing gum we might get, and roll it into a ball, as well as scour the creek banks and trash heaps for metal parts and save them all for the scrap man who came each month. Women were expected to keep the family together and take one of the jobs left open by the men leaving for war.

I remember stories of Mom travelling by train to see my dad in Texas when he was in basic training. I can see her, at about twenty one, beautiful in a suggestive, sultry, Gene Tierney way; dressed to the nines, long dark hair in place with old-fashioned *rats* in back, wearing white gloves, seamed stockings and heels, her green eyes taking in the sights, excited to be on a train going somewhere, anywhere away from West Virginia. She hadn't yet committed to enrolling in cosmetology school. I wonder if she planned to discuss it with my dad or had she already figured out that it's easier to apologize after the fact than try to get approval up front. On this trip, she would have had few, if any, worries, knowing the two grandmothers were caring for my younger brother, Danny, and me. And knowing they'd keep us if she did decide to go to school.

I can imagine my father's deep feeling on her arrival—relief that she had come and a slight pressure to make this the perfect visit for her. I wonder if they had moments of passion or love in those early days. Was she excited to see him, after months apart, or was she just excited to be travelling?

He always wanted her, from the day they met until the day he died, even though both married other people after their own two divorces from each other. They would have married each other a third time, but my mother missed the bus. My father had warned her: "Be on that bus from Florida, or else."

She missed the bus, and my father had finally had enough. He went on and married his pregnant girl friend, a good woman who had four or five kids of her own, and who could pass for my mother's twin. But, I digress.

In the early days, my father had found the patience to wait out my mother for nearly three years before marrying her. After all, she was young, and he wanted to show himself as a loyal, respectable, middle-class suitor who offered her a way up and out of her very questionable background. He saw her fragility and wanted to show her she could count on him.

He also wanted to win my mother's love, a formidable task.

As mother had said, once Granny Bill checked out Millard French Steele, Jr., she made it clear no one else could come courting. My dad had a job, came from a good family, and was respectful to Granny. That's all she needed to know.

My mother said he was the first person to make her feel special.

"He never tried to force himself on me and he treated me like I was somebody."

Truth is, there weren't many choices for a girl of her background, up and around the hollows and low bottoms of Logan County. The county was known mostly for its violence, its poverty, and coal wars during the struggle to unionize the mines. It was the final resting place of Anderson "Anse" Hatfield, and, with his many children scattered around the county, talk of the feud came easy.

My mother was exceptionally beautiful, with a thin frame, a head full of curly, auburn hair, green eyes. Her features were dramatic and sharp, whereas Granny and her people were more rounded, as if farming, and poverty and hard work had worn down their edges. Mother had a hint of sexuality about her, even at thirteen. Living in a rough-edged environment of illicit booze and sex, honky tonk music and romantic notions, she had many reasons for attaching herself to my father at the time, not the least of which was my grandmother.

In 1935, Granny Bill was a demanding mother with little time and hardly an ounce of nurturing for her thirteen year old daughter. She knew more about making money than mothering. Throughout the Depression, she had taken on responsibilities for her several siblings and extended relatives, most of them scratch farmers or disabled miners and World War I veterans. They all relied on her and, in return, did various jobs for her when required.

Although Granny completed only the third grade, she was as smart and cunning a business person as Leona Helmsley or Donald Trump, and she was used to getting what she wanted. Some of the things she wanted required skimming the law—paying off sheriffs and judges, buying and hauling votes, selling whiskey under the counter to known customers, and shuttling moonshine from the hills up to Chicago's speakeasies. She was always finding ways to bring in a few more dollars, including, my mother once told me, being madam of a house with a few working girls when times were *really* hard.

"I'd heard so many stories about what these girls did, when I was little," Mother said. "I was afraid to touch the doorknobs of their rooms, afraid I'd catch something. But your granny made me get in there and clean their rooms. I was scared to death."

"A girl's got to make a living!" Granny would say, referring to herself and the even poorer girls who counted on her. Shaking her head as if to say *life is hard; life isn't fair,* she'd go on about her business, without judgment, not caring what others thought.

In those early days, long before I was born, business and survival came first and, when necessary, Granny would assign my mother to various family members for care or get one of *her girls* to keep an eye on her. The girls might be part-time waitresses at the beer garden, part-time prostitutes whose looks enabled them to have a job, or just young pregnant girls who'd been disowned or left behind. Granny took them all in and gave them a new start.

She gave them a roof over their heads, small change to buy what they needed. She scheduled doctors' appointments and intervened with boyfriends from time to time. Everyone around knew they could count on *Aunt Billie*. She was family to many who depended on her. The hard times called for the kind of extended family support structure she could provide, one helping another. Everyone also knew there'd be no foolishness with Billie or her daughter, or they'd be in for one hell of a time.

For young Melba Brownie, that was far from enough to make her feel valued, much less loved.

"They worked me hard, treated me like I was the help, not family," Mom told me.

"They sent me to stay and work like a dog for Aunt Stella and her husband, Andy Johnson, at their grocery store or to help Aunt Helen at her Purple H Beer Garden in Switzer. Nobody showed any affection. It was all work. Your granny wasn't around much. And then there was that time that Andy tried to corner me. I had to fight for myself all the time."

I've tried, without success, to reconcile my Granny's not being a good mother to my mom with my own experience as her granddaughter. She was a perfect grandmother, to my way of thinking. She was also unlike any person I'd ever met. Strong and decisive don't begin to describe her.

My mind can accept my mother's unhappy stories, but not my heart. I adored Granny Bill and never doubted her love for me.

I asked Mom once if she ever told Granny about Andy. She said no, she was too afraid to tell her, afraid she'd be blamed for it.

Always insecure, feeling unwanted and out of place growing up, somehow my mother knew she didn't belong where she'd landed on this earth.

Mother at 14, 1936.
With Granny Bill
at Natural Bridge, Va

The Mountains and the Coal Camps

The mountains in Logan County, West Virginia, were close, as close as light to shade. Only creeks and rivers, hardtop roads and occasional wide, loamy bottoms and coal camps could force their way between them. Wide spots in the road. My dad always said: "Everything happens in the wide spots in the road." He would also remind us that any day he saw three hours of sunshine was a good day, a damned good day. It wasn't much of an exaggeration. He worked the early shift in #4 mine in Stirrat at the time. Leaving the house around 5:30 in the morning, he seldom got home before 4 p.m. Shorter days in winter cut the sunlight by half, and he'd often curse the mountains for depriving us of light.

Unlike my dad, I thought of the mountains as magical. I'd spend full days exploring them whenever I could. High mountains, but not so high you couldn't climb them on a hot, muggy summer day or when they were brushed with shades of orange and yellow and a red so bright, it looked like the woods were in flames. I was drawn to the mountains where my imagination flourished, where I felt safe, where there were no harsh words, no bitterness.

Underneath the shade of sycamore and chinquapin oak trees, I'd play and dream and build fortresses among purple asters and wild columbine. I could see three or four mountains to the south and west. The sun would creep down one hill, linger for a few hours in the valley, and, before I knew it, start its climb up toward me or the next hill over. I'd sit for hours, looking, listening, inhaling the place. A fragrance of honeysuckle and Sweet William prevailed over that of the rotting leaves underneath. White mushrooms bent this way and that around the base of trees; clusters of grayish oyster mushrooms stacked up along the sides of rotten trunks. Sunlight filtered through the branches of young trees in wide streams of light.

According to Granny, who seemed to know everything, our forest was a young one; the older trees had been removed for timber to construct the coal camps or lay railroad ties at the turn of the century. Somehow, the hills seemed older, ancient even, with a beauty and quiet that only jays or crows or blowing leaves dared interrupt. The silence of that space filled me and cleansed away any hurt or disappointment I had at the time. Being in those hills also inspired an aesthetic and a curiosity that has characterized most of my life.

Granny and I walked the hills together just for the joy of it. So much to be discovered! Fossils of seashells, Indian arrowheads, wild blooming plants like chokeberry and spiderwort. I took bark and leaves and flowers back to the house, careful not to tear them, and pressed them in a special book, writing down the names Granny always knew. She pointed out plants that were poisonous and those that Indians and the *old timers* had used as medicine. Strange rock formations in the mountains made me wonder whether they'd settled here during the Ice Age or were carved by alien visitors. I preferred the alien version and, at night, lying in the yard, staring up at the dark sky, tried to imagine what it was like up there.

Occasionally we found carvings thought to be discarded by Indian tribes, and I was filled with ideas about their life here in my valley. Had they eaten nuts and berries from these same trees? Had they slept here, where I sat and dreamed my future?

I liked to imitate what I thought the Indians would do, picking huckleberries, painting my face and whoo-hooing through the woods, as I listened to Granny's stories. She told me she had come to West Virginia around 1907 as a young girl with her family, travelling from the Shenandoah Valley over the Alleghenies, in a covered wagon. Her older sister, Helen, had come before them and settled in Logan County. Her brothers, still in their teens, saw a future in the mines.

"They weren't no jobs down in Meadow View; just people farming and growing tobacco, raising cows for market. None of the boys liked farm work, so, when I was seven, Daddy packed us all up in the wagon and we came across the mountains to West Virginia. Momma died when I was fourteen and I had to raise the younger ones. Then daddy married Nellie and they had more babies. I raised 'em all." She didn't seem to resent this; it just was the way things were.

As we walked in the woods together, she would tell more stories about her family, her half-brothers and sisters, distant relatives I would meet only at family funerals. I wanted to know everything.

Granny knew about the Indians and told me the county of Logan was named for an important Iroquois chief. She explained how the Iroquois and Delaware and Shawnee had hunted the area a hundred or more years ago and said they had no concept of private property as applied to the land. The land belonged to all of them, she said, and they shared hunting rights in this area.

That idea stuck in my mind, because I knew Granny Bill owned a lot of land here in Sarah Ann, our little wide spot in the road. Her land included a couple of hills and the broad bottom at the foot of the hill, edged by Island Creek. As we'd come down the hill, we could see in the distance her beer garden and motel, looking small, like pictures in the books I read. Unlike the Indians, Granny and her people thought owning land was very important.

This area of Logan County was famous for the Hatfield-McCoy feud, even though most of the fighting took place in Kentucky, along the Tug River. Clan leader Anderson Hatfield—Devil Anse—owned these hills then and had a thriving timber business. In his later days, he retired to a small cabin down in this bottom and he died here. Granny knew lots about the Hatfields and told me that Devil Anse's funeral was the largest ever held in Logan County. She bought this land from one of his relatives. (See copy of original deed.)

Learning about the feud and how Devil Anse himself had lived here—right where Granny's beer garden was now—intensified my love of this place. It was an important place; famous people had settled here. Granny had pictures of those times and those people all over the walls of her beer garden, and sometimes, strangers, driving through to the county seat, would stop to look at the pictures, having heard of the feud and the graveyard down the way.

The Hatfield graveyard, with its life-sized, Carrara marble statue of Devil Anse, stood above the clearing on the next mountain over and attracted a few tourists now and then. Granny tried for years to get the county to clean up the graveyard and turn it into a tourist spot, but they never did. Travelers had to pass a No Trespassing sign, cross a concrete bridge, push aside all the overgrown brush and fallen tree limbs and climb the rocky hill to get a close look. The monument was tall enough for us to see it from the porch over the beer garden, and Granny used to say the old Devil liked to come down at night and scare little kids who'd been misbehaving.

Walking these woods and wide spots in the road with Granny, I learned to respect the land and our history: the significance of the mountains that bound us, where family came from, and who'd been here before us. I worried, later on, if my mother ever minded growing up in Hatfield country, on Hatfield land, given her own connection to the McCoys.

Halfway between the county seat of Logan and Granny's beer garden, the space between the mountains widened to make room for the unincorporated town of Omar, a coal camp built by West Virginia Coal and Coke, later owned by Island Creek Coal.

Coal camps. Where coal was exhumed from the hollows that cut into the narrow valley; where the company owned everything in sight; where railroad tracks were laid for long trains carrying coal to the cities, to rivers and barges. Logan County was notorious for the civil uprisings between miners and company detectives on Blair Mountain in the early 1920's, and, in the 40's and and 50's, was one of the most productive coal mining areas in the state. The demand for coal was more than locals could fulfill, and coal companies resorted to recruiting men as they got off the boat at Ellis Island.

Hungarians, Polish, Italians and more had come for a better life in this country. The company put them all on trains and busses and sent them into the isolation of West Virginia. They brought their rich cultures and customs and language into the hills. They also crawled into the open mine faces, lay on their backs and sides, and used pick axes to loosen coal from the seam, only to have it shoveled onto low, flat railway cars by the men behind them. Going deeper, following the seam, counting on each other to keep it safe, most of the men's lives were spent in darkness. Color made no difference in the mines. Not color, not nationality, for the men all depended on each other for their lives.

Coal camps. Small, unincorporated towns in the meager flat land, where everything is built, owned and run by the coal company—schools, churches, stores, theatres, and homes available for rent. Coal camps like Omar connected to other unincorporated towns by a single blacktop road that led to the county seat. Wide spaces like Crystal Block, population of about eighty in the 1930's and 40's, with a company store and post office; Sarah Ann with two beer gardens, a grocery store and Freewill Baptist Church for the few residents; Delbarton, home of a well-established red light district, near the town of Williamson, with approximately seventy nine residents. All experienced the boom and bust days of the 1930's, 40's and 50's.

Away from the tracks, in the main section of Omar, were the spacious homes and yards for the supervisors' and managers' families. Many were Catholic and attended what we called *fancy* churches in downtown Logan, whereas most workers' families attended Freewill Baptist, Church of God, or Community Methodist Churches in the camps. Children in the miners' housing developments were generally free to play together despite differences in race and national origin. The bigger dividing line was between miners' children and those of the company management. With few exceptions, these children were sent away to private schools in the fall, and we'd see them on their spacious porches only in summertime.

Omar, like all of West Virginia, had features in common with both the North and the South in the way it treated race. Segregated schools and public facilities, including the movie theater, the restaurant and pool hall, were a fact of life.

But life underground was something else.

My family spent many years in one coal town or another, relying on the company doctor when one of us was sick or buying our clothes and groceries with script at the company store. Script was advance pay that could be spent at company-owned stores and deducted from the miner's paycheck on payday. For a dime I could see my favorite cowboys chase each other on the movie screen. Blacks, upstairs; whites, downstairs. Besides the company store, Omar had a post office and small restaurant; a couple of churches, and two schools: one for whites, one for blacks. Not much more.

Along lower Main Street, fronting the tracks, were the small five-room, identical stucco duplexes set aside for section bosses' and miners' families. Black dust blew off the coal cars as they passed, putting down layers of gloom everywhere: on the shared, small porches and windows of these duplexes, on the clothes hanging on the line, on toys left out overnight. It irritated my mother to no end. We were always scrubbing the windows and porch floor but made little progress for long. An alleyway ran behind the duplexes, then another row of houses, where my best friend, Mildred, lived. The alleyway where we played was our main escape from parents.

Across the road and railroad tracks, cut into sides of the mountain, were long and narrow wooden *shotgun* houses where blacks lived; the houses lined up in rows with outhouses to the side.

Life in Omar was organized, with days assigned to major housekeeping chores. This seemed to be an unspoken agreement. If it were Monday, women did laundry and hung the clothes out to dry. Tuesdays, all the laundry had to be sprinkled down, rolled up, and placed in a basket with a heavy towel covering it. Wednesday was for ironing, lest clothes get musty-smelling or mildewed. Being something of a perfectionist as a housekeeper, my mother swept the kitchen, vacuumed the entire house, and shook out the rugs every day of the week except Sundays. My mother was an impeccable housekeeper, and she'd threaten my brother and me with a spanking if we stepped on one of the shag rugs after she'd cleaned. We had to walk around them.

On Saturdays, everyone dressed up to go to town. Children polished their shoes; men wore hats; and proper women, like my mother aspired to be, wouldn't be seen without their white cotton gloves or nylon stockings. We always ran into someone we knew at the Dime Store or Franklin's Drug Store or the Piggly Wiggly.

While Mom and I shopped, Dad spent Saturday mornings at The Smoke House, drinking coffee and talking with other miners and supervisors who did the same. The Smoke House restaurant was the informal political headquarters for local gentry and men affiliated with the mines. It's where my dad traded stories with mine officials in hopes of keeping his job as section boss or, better yet, moving up to a position of federal safety inspector. The Smoke House catered to men, and gossip was rampant as to what took place upstairs, on the second floor.

Granny's half-sister, Pauline, had the inside, true story. She worked as a waitress downstairs for many years and knew what the lawyers, judges, and mine officials were headed for as they climbed the worn stairs to the second floor of the restaurant. A few games of Saturday poker, some shots of whiskey, political deals, and heavily made-up women in tight dresses left little to the imagination. Just another day in Logan County, according to Aunt Pauline.

Evenings, after a couple of beers, Pauline would have us all gasping and giggling at her stories about Logan County's so-called elite and pious church-goers. Granny encouraged her talk, as she knew best how and when to use this information to get what she wanted. Yes, just another day in a wide spot in the road.

Anderson
"Devil Anse" Hatfield

The Memorial in Sarah Ann

The Hatfield Family

Members of the clan with Devil Anse - Ock Damron,
Jim Vance, W.B. Borden
(WV State Archives)

It wasn't until May 1976 that Hatfields and the McCoys publicly buried the hatchet. Jimmy McCoy, (left) then 91, and Willis Hatfield, 88, met in Hardy, Ky., to end the hostilities their fathers had participated in. Both of the elderly patriarchs have since died. This portrait of the Hatfield clan (below) in April 1897 resembles a reunion of soldiers more than a family get-together. But those were fighting days and for about 15 years the Hatfields slugged it out with the McCoys in the Appalachians. The bloodshed reportedly began when tipsy members of both families clashed on an election day.

The Associated Press

For Belley Garten

Anderson Hatfield & Lewey Hatfield
his wife
To: Dee
James E Price, Trustee
Date of Deed 9th April 1889.
all coal oil & gas salt water
& other Minerals
with the the right to remove
the same, and to use all
rock timber or any material
necessary in the removal
thereof.
Hatfield reserved the free use
of all coal for domestic use
and it was agreed in said
deed that if the Co. desired to use
the surface with in 5 years
on any of the Francey that they
would pay anse $10 per acer
any within 300 feet of his house
* cleared land they would pay
$20. per acre, but the time
for they run out there is now
no reservation on the surface
any price the owner may see
fit to require the coal Co to
pay. He cleared 82 acres

*Anderson (Devil Anse) Hatfield and his wife Levicy deeded
67.57 acres of land along Island Creek to Myrtle Farley on
April 9, 1889. On 13 February 1939, Myrtle Farley signed
over this deed to Granny Bill (Billy Gartin). The deed explains
the right to coal, gas and water on the property.
Purchase price was $20 per acre.*

32

Billie Brown's Back in Town

1920's and '30's

When the 18th Amendment to the U.S. Constitution declared in 1920 there would be no sale, manufacturing or distribution of alcohol, Granny saw a great business opportunity.

"A girl's gotta make a living somehow," Granny always said. "It's the government made criminals of bootleggers."

In spite of the prohibition law, the drinkers didn't stop drinking. They just worked around the rules, managing to find speakeasies where they knew someone or poor people who'd sell them a jar of lightnin' here and there. There was no shortage of drinkers.

In the middle of Prohibition, with Black Tuesday and the onset of the Great Depression heaping coals on the fire, Granny's people were hard hit: they had to make a living or die trying. Several of her kin—from down in western Virginia, near the Tennessee border, and those who lived up in the hollows in Logan County—had learned from their fathers and grandfathers how to make moonshine, a common practice among the Scotch-Irish who settled the area in the 18th and 19th centuries.

Poor people needed a drink now and then just like the rich folks, Granny would say.

Long before I was born, bootlegging moonshine was a family business for Granny and my great uncles and aunts. Some made it and hauled it out of the mountains. Others drove or delivered it throughout the back roads of Logan County and beyond.

Granny managed the operation, which means she collected the money and, when it came to deliveries outside West Virginia, she was the one in charge. Through assorted distant relatives in Appalachia, she also had secured license plates from several states—Kentucky, Ohio, Illinois and Virginia among them—providing easy passage without drawing attention of the revenuers, government agents responsible for halting the distilling or "bootlegging" of alcohol.

With the smarts of a grifter, Granny used Prohibition to her advantage, keeping her family and many others out of the poor house for years. She understood people—what they wanted and what they were made of—which enabled her to best the bettors and fool the revenue men.

She'd never talk about those days with me, but answer my inquiries with, "Oh, them's just stories. Don't pay no attention."

Other relatives, however, could be encouraged to tell the stories. They were much more interesting than the *Bobbsey Twins* books I borrowed from the school library or even the *Crime Magazines* I found under Granny's mattress. This was real stuff: hiding out, keeping one step ahead of the law, being chased, outsmarting the feds. I was fascinated and proud of her.

Never a thought about this being wrong or illegal. After all, I'd seen this kind of behavior in the movies.

Granny loved movies and, as a child, I was her most frequent companion. We watched westerns and *shoot-'em-up* crime stories, and once she took me to see *Gun Crazy*, a precursor of *Bonnie and Clyde*. I was as crazy about the movies as she was, and loved the excitement of brazen women outsmarting the men and keeping a few steps ahead of the law. For as little as a dime, we could experience a whole different world on the screen. As I heard the stories of her younger, bootlegging days, I imagined her as one of these super stars. I was proud of her past escapades.

I'm told that once, when she and her older sister, Helen, were trying to outrun the revenue men, they stopped their souped-up "shine" car, grabbed their extra license plates and ran down some railroad tracks, stuffing the plates into their bras and panties as they ran. The license plates were valuable and had to be saved, as they gave them the freedom to travel into Ohio and Illinois and not be flagged as someone from out of state, a "shiner."

This particular time, the revenuers saw the car, pulled over, and started chasing the two flappers down the tracks.

"Slow 'em down!" Granny is said to have yelled to her sister, and they began to take off their watches and jewelry, hold them in the air and throw them onto the tracks. It slowed the revenuers down, all right; they'd much rather have the valuables than try to arrest one more bootlegger!

Granny's work took her to Chicago frequently, where she enjoyed the company of bar owners, mobsters and hotel concierges alike. Rumor has it that Helen's son, Preston, was part of Al Capone's *Murder, Incorporated*, a name given by the press to organized crime groups such as Capone's gang. But this rumor has never been verified in any way.

Granny and Helen once took my five-year-old mother to the big city and, to hear my mother tell it, my grandmother wore long, beaded gowns to high-style, high-swinging parties where black jazz musicians mixed in with the white crowd. A natural born wheeler-dealer, Granny enjoyed giving the drinkers what they wanted, loved the excitement and parties in Chicago, while tucking a substantial amount of their money in her ample bosom.

The image of her in the midst of this fast-paced society, making her own way, seemed so exciting to me as a young girl. It fueled my imagination and my desire to experience a larger world, outside of Sarah Ann, West Virginia. If she could do it, why couldn't I?

There were very few stories about Granny's first husband, Chester Brownie, who was with her off and on during these years. All that people would say is that he went out for razor blades one day and never came back. He was around long enough to get her pregnant, but their son, Arthur, died in infancy around 1921. I've often wondered if she had been sad about his death. How would it have changed her life if he had lived? Was it this loss that contributed to her need for excitement and her willingness to take such big risks? Did she really not care what others thought?

Some time after Chester Brownie disappeared, Granny dropped the "ie" from her last name, for reasons unknown to me. Everyone who knew her in the late 1920's and thereafter called her Billie Brown, until she remarried in the 1940's—to another Chester—and took her new husband's last name, Gartin.

No matter; most people I knew in the 1940's and '50's still called her, Billie Brown.

Granny managed to escape the revenuers many times, once by diverting mash from the moonshine still into the pigs' pen, so the smell was camouflaged.

My mother recalled times when her Uncle Charlie would come get her out of grade school, take her home, remove one of the planks from over the stairs, and slide her down under the steps so she could pull out pints and half-pints for another haul.

"I was small enough to get in there," Mother would laugh when telling the tale. Later on, she admitted it made her feel special and needed, something very important to her.

I may have grown up in a part of the country where Hatfield and McCoy lore ran deep, but nothing was more exciting to me than Granny's early life.

Ultimately, in 1930, when my mother was eight years old, Granny was caught and sentenced to a year at the brand-new Alderson Federal Prison for Women, in the foothills of the Allegheny Mountains, near the Greenbrier River.

Years later, I read that most of the inmates housed in the dormitories of this minimum-security facility were relatives of famous mobsters and grandmotherly women who robbed or embezzled money from banks during the Depression. Granny admitted from time to time that she had learned a lot from the women at Alderson. That's all she'd say. Nothing specific.

It made me wonder what she did learn. Did she learn about the intricacies of robbing banks? How to deal with lawmen and lawyers? Did the women housed there share their escapades or trade secrets? I wonder about the pecking order of women in that prison; who was in charge? Did Granny boss around people there, just as she did in real life? The women at Alderson weren't pushovers, and I can only imagine the stories, the cunning and intrigue they shared.

It never bothered me that she'd been in prison. After all, she got out, just like the women in the movies we'd seen. According to my mother, Granny came out of Alderson in style, wearing a new suit and hat she'd made in one of the prison training classes.

Headlines in *The Logan Banner* read, "Billie Brown's Back in Town."

Granny Bill

Getting to the Truth of Things

1946, West Virginia to Boone, N.C.

It was common knowledge that in 1922 Granny went to visit her father on his farm outside Abingdon and returned with a baby girl. As one great-aunt explained years later, "Billie never did give no explanation. You couldn't ask her about it or she'd get mad. She'd just say, 'she's my baby,' and that was that."

The whispers and raised eyebrows among Granny's siblings, plus the fear of Granny's looming death, must have given my 23-year-old mother courage she'd never had before, because one day she decided to find out the facts of her parenthood once and for all.

I didn't witness the confrontation and couldn't hear much of it, either, as there were two or three grown-ups with their ears to the door.

They scattered when the door opened. Mom came out of the room, shoulders back, her face puffed with red blotches. She grabbed my hand and told me to pick up my books; we were going home. That evening as I was showering with her, she told me Granny wasn't her real mother. I remember it as if it were yesterday.

I said, "I knew that."

She picked me up and shook me.

"What are you saying? How did you know that?"

I told her I'd heard it from Granny's sisters. She put me down and leaned her forehead against the shower wall for what seemed a long time, just shaking her head. Looking back, I don't remember any discussion of the situation after that and it easily left my mind. It didn't make sense to me anyway.

I knew Granny Bill was my grandmother, and that's all that mattered to me.

A few days later, just after my fifth birthday, my mother told my four-year-old brother, Danny, and me we were going on a road trip to North Carolina with Granny Bill. I was excited! We'd never traveled so far away before, and I had decided already I wanted to visit all forty eight states by the time I grew up. This trip would add North Carolina to Virginia, West Virginia, and Tennessee!

Danny cried that he didn't want to go 'cause he always got carsick.

"You're going," my mother said, "so straighten up and fly right."

I sat on the edge of her bed hugging the books I wanted to take with me, afraid to ask questions or make a wrong move. I watched as she ironed one of my best dresses and put it in the suitcase next to her own. Her mouth was tight and I could see her jaw clench and unclench as she applied white liquid shoe polish to Danny's shoes before putting them in a side pocket of the borrowed, green Samsonite bag.

That particular car trip and the night in the motel are gone from my memory completely, but our arrival into the outskirts of Boone, North Carolina remains vivid.

Granny pulled the car into a short driveway that was blocked by a latched gate and cow fencing that surrounded several acres of land. Off to the right, on a slight hill, was a modest, white, Victorian house with a wrap-around porch.

"Now what do we do?" my mother asked nervously, tapping her ruby-red fingernails on the dashboard.

"We wait," Granny said, her hands gripping the steering wheel. "She'll see us; she'll come down."

"I suppose you worked all this out on the telephone."

"We'll just wait right here. She'll be down."

"Well, I'm not sitting in this hot car." Mother opened the door on her side, got out, and leaned against the fender, shielding her eyes from the sun while looking up at the house.

"You kids get out and pick some wildflowers for the lady," my grandmother said.

"And don't get dirty," my mother threw over her shoulder.

"Who is this lady?" Danny asked.

"Just a friend of mine; you've never met her," was all my grandmother said.

Once out of the car, I started picking dandelions, white daisies, and whatever wildflowers grew along the road, wrapping the stems in a silver gum wrapper I'd found in the driveway. Danny went around the car to stand beside Mother.

Within a few minutes, a tall, dark-haired woman in a pink house dress came off the porch and started down the unpaved driveway. Granny Bill went over to the gate and nodded hello. The two of them talked for a few minutes, while Danny climbed on the wooden support of the gate and tried to get it to swing.

Granny's lady friend unlatched the gate, and she and Granny walked around to where my mother had just stomped out her cigarette. I kept picking flowers, trying to ease closer and hear the conversation, when Granny said, "Bring Mrs. McCoy the flowers you've picked for her; we're going up to the house."

Mrs. McCoy's living room had the tallest ceilings I'd ever seen, with lots of curved, white wood around the tops of the walls and all the furniture arranged to face a large pipe organ with three keyboards and wooden foot pedals.

"Don't touch anything," my mother whispered sharply as I turned a full circle looking at everything.

"Do you play, ma'am?" I asked Mrs. McCoy.

Handing me a glass of lemonade, she bent down as if to study me, and allowed that she played for their church.

"Would you play for us?"

"Leave her be, young lady," my grandmother said. "It's too hot. Now take your drink outside on the porch; you too, Danny."

I sat in the swing awhile, finished my lemonade, then hung over the railings and looked around. Having left my books in the car, I was bored and restless but didn't want to leave the shade of the porch, so I pulled petals from the daisies that had been laid on the wicker table to the side of the door.

It seemed an awful long time before the three grown-ups came out.

"Thank Mrs. McCoy for the lemonade," Granny Bill called out. "Now, go get in the car."

Mrs. McCoy smiled and waved to us as we ran toward the gate, and I heard her say something about a getting a picture. As

I climbed into the back seat, I could see Granny Bill handing a Brownie camera back to her friend, who kissed my mother on the cheek, turned quickly, and went inside the house.

No one talked much after we were settled in the car and on the road. Mom was looking out the side window, her arms crossed over her chest. Granny had both hands on the wheel, her fingers moving nervously, as if she were tapping out a song. I kept quiet, while Danny cuddled up with a pillow in the corner of the back seat.

After a while, I noticed my mother wiping her eyes with a handkerchief. Granny reached over and patted her arm and said something I couldn't understand. I sat with my head leaning on the back of mother's seat, to better hear their soft talk. Only once did my mother raise her voice. She cursed God's name and said, "Why didn't you tell me? Why did you leave me wondering all these years?"

She made a loud sound, like a dog moaning, while Granny kept saying, "Honey, I just thought it best not to go into it. We can't change the way things are. Hattie's a good woman; she just couldn't handle another baby at the time."

I was puzzled. I'd known Granny Bill all my life. How could my mother have two mothers? But here they were saying it was so. Part of me wanted to comfort my mother, but I didn't know how. I didn't want this Mrs. Hattie McCoy to be my grandmother.

I sat back in my seat and turned my head to look for cows in the pastures or license plates from out of state, games my granny had taught me to keep from getting sick in the car.

Mrs. Hattie McCoy,
my mother's biological mother

Christmas Revelations

1947, Beckley, West Virginia

When my dad returned from World War II in 1946, I'm told he considered using the GI Bill for college but decided against it. After all, he had a wife and two children to support. Knowing what I know now, my father could have succeeded at whatever field he chose. I can imagine my mother encouraging him to go to college—if for no other reason than it would require him to be away, out of town. There was no college within a 60-mile radius of Logan. Secondly, his being away in school would free her to work and be more independent. She could always count on his mother, my Granny Steele, to care for the children.

Mom completed a program in cosmetology while Dad was overseas, a period she often, publicly, described as her happiest. Before Dad came home, she worked briefly as a beautician in Logan and enjoyed being out and sociable. Above all, Mother didn't want to be stuck in the house with two children.

Once Dad came home, he put his foot down.

"No wife of mine is going to have to work."

Despite her resistance and strong will, she gave in and quit her job. He already knew he had to keep a close eye on her.

Like his father and older brother before him, my dad became a coal miner. The changing, post-war economy had brought boom times to Logan County, but they were interspersed with closings brought about by efforts to unionize the mines.

A company in Beckley, West Virginia hired Dad and a few others from Logan County to work their mines while West Virginia Coal and Coke closed, due to conflicts about safety rules and pay scales. I often heard my parents talk about the importance of the union, and everyone we knew had a photo of the United Mine Workers' John L. Lewis on a shelf somewhere in their house.

Beckley sat down low in a valley where the Appalachians softened toward the Blue Ridge Mountains. I don't remember moving there, but it is where most of my memories start, on a sloping hill among the working class town folk.

To entertain ourselves, my five-year-old brother and I tagged along after the older kids or dug for treasure in our back yard. None of the children I played with then has a name or face now.

During that first summer, my dad helped me with my coloring, teaching me to stay in the lines and to think about whether green and purple were the best colors for the elephant. Never having seen an elephant, I argued the colors seemed just right to me, and he laughingly agreed. He and I often sat on the cool living room floor in the evenings to color or practice writing, with Danny playing with tinker toys nearby, and my mom making cornbread and beans or potato pancakes in the kitchen.

Dad encouraged me to practice writing my name on the lined paper he'd brought home, showing me how to use the blue sharpener to get the number two pencil point just right.

"Not too sharp, now; it'll just break off. That's good."

I was serious about learning to write my name before school started. Very serious. I bore down on pencils as if I could force words out of them.

"Take it easy. Not so much pressure," my dad would say. He'd take my hand and shake it slightly to make it relax.

"Try again." he'd say, gentle and patient with me.

One time, when I made a mistake, I was so angry that I nearly tore the eraser off the pencil, trying to correct it. I pressed so hard, the paper ripped. Even then, I knew words had power and I needed to get them right.

He lifted my hand and said, "Go easy. Be gentle. It'll work better that way."

And it did. And it does.

Why do I remember this? The memory cuts deep.

I was both ready and scared to start school in the fall of 1947. I'd heard all the first graders got to color and write words and read books and then come home and eat cookies their mothers made. I liked the whole idea. But I knew I'd miss my brother, and I *really* knew he'd miss me.

"Sissy don't have to go to school," he'd whisper in his sweet, sad, five-year-old voice, day after day after day.

"But I do. It's the law."

"Mommy don't go to school."

"Well, I have to go. It'll be fun and I'll tell you everything when I come home."

"Sissy don't *have* to go to school," he'd repeat.

I went off to school that fall, leaving my frail, blond-headed brother crying behind me. My dad stayed home so that Mom could take me to my first-grade class.

All the mothers lined up against the classroom wall and watched while their babies found chairs and crayons and friends or otherwise clung tightly to their skirts as if there were a ghost in the room. The teacher's job was to coax all of us to a seat and table. As I remember it, I was cautious but easily persuaded. Some of us wanted our mothers to stay, but, slowly, as we were brought into the excitement of our first day in school, we barely noticed the mothers slipping out of the room.

Someone—I don't know who—came to pick me up at the end of the day. As we skipped down my street, I could see Danny sitting on the front steps, bouncing his ball, waiting for me. The minute he saw me, he raced out of the yard, jumping up and down.

"Sissy's home. Sissy's home!"

A perfect day. I couldn't wait to tell him all the things I'd learned while I was away.

In December, around Christmas time, snow piled up nearly to window level, and Danny and I both got the mumps. We were quarantined to our small bedroom. The shades were pulled and we were told, if we turned on the lights, we'd go blind.

In no uncertain terms, my mother told us to stay in bed and not come out.

It was breathlessly boring and I remember sleeping a lot. When awake, Danny and I would talk about our favorite cowboys and what we hoped Santa would bring us in a few days.

One night I woke up hearing my dad in the kitchen. He was whistling and making noise with the pots and pans. I looked over at

Danny, three feet away in his bed, sound asleep. I walked to the door that connected to the kitchen and called out, "Daddy!"

"Get back in that bed, little girl. You're not supposed to be up."

"What are you doing?"

"Nothing that concerns you. Go back to bed."

I punched Danny as I passed his bed, and sat square in the middle of mine.

"Daddy, I smell something."

"You just stay where you are."

The syrupy smell of bubbling sugar and peanut butter that stole under the door into our room could mean only one thing: he was making peanut butter fudge, my favorite. My dad was excellent at making candy.

"Where's mommy?" I yelled.

"Went to the store. She'll be back soon."

I lay down and yelled at Danny to wake up, happy in knowing what was about to happen.

Soon enough, I saw the kitchen light go out and heard my dad walking toward our door. "Don't tell your mother, now. She'll kill me if she knows I'm giving you candy at night."

"We won't, we won't," we assured him, picking out the largest square we could see or feel in the dark.

"Now, go to sleep."

"Thank you, Daddy."

Later that night, much later, a noise woke me. A quiet noise, like a cat crying. But we didn't have a cat. I looked over at Danny, sleeping. Not even a purr. Again, the noise.

Maybe a baby crying, I thought? But whose baby could it be? Did my parents have company? I slipped over to the second door in our room, the one that separated our bedroom from our parents' room, and listened.

Again, a small cry.

Accepting that I might go blind, I put my eye to the keyhole. I could see my mother sitting at her vanity, her face in her hands, rocking back and forth.

Something must have hurt her, I thought. I pushed open the door and raced to her side of the room. She pulled me close and cried for the longest time.

I was shocked; I didn't know mothers cried.

"What's wrong, Mommy? Are you hurt?"

"No, no, no." She shook her head, wiped her eyes.

"I'm not hurt, honey. Your daddy's just mad at me. Just promise me that if something happens to me and your daddy, you'll stay with me."

I didn't know what she meant. What could happen?

"Mommy, I . . ."

"Your daddy's mad because he thinks I was flirting with some man I met," she started crying again, "and he said he'd take you and Danny away from me if I didn't stop. Promise me you'll never leave me."

I couldn't answer. What was she saying? Why would I leave her? I felt weak from having lain in bed for so long. This was too much to comprehend.

She pulled me onto her lap, rocking me back and forth, saying if I went with my dad, I'd have a mean stepmother like Cinderella.

"You don't want that, do you, honey?"

I wasn't sure exactly how all this could come about, but I had the sense to know I didn't want a mean stepmother like Cinderella.

I don't remember how I answered her, or even if I did. I was out of my body, where flashing lights flooded my brain, numbing my thoughts. My heart was stilled by what she was saying.

Out of the corner of my eye, I saw my father on the front porch, flicking a cigarette toward the road and turning toward the door. I saw my own reflection in the vanity mirror and was surprised, for I couldn't feel my own body.

"Get back to bed before he sees you. And don't say anything to your father about this. It's our secret, okay?"

I lay in my bed, wishing Danny awake, without any luck. I couldn't even call my brother's name. I had no words. I just wished and wished he would know I needed him and wake up and bring me back. Mother's secret seemed much bigger than Daddy's with the candy, but I couldn't make sense of it. Daddy wouldn't leave us; what was she talking about?

Somehow, finally, not hearing any more noise, I fell asleep, wondering if things would be the same tomorrow.

The next day was Christmas, and we were allowed out of the bedroom, because, they said, Santa had brought something for us. Neither parent seemed out of sorts, which made me wonder what exactly had happened in the night. Mother chided me for being so fussy and not eating the breakfast she had made.

"You'd better eat if you want to see what Santa brought!"

No recognition of our exchange, as if nothing had happened.

Santa brought Danny a boxing set, with shiny, red, padded boxing gloves and a ball attached by a flexible rod to a metal stand. Danny was so weak from being in bed for a week, he could barely stand up, but he was determined to get the Joe Louis gloves on his tiny hands. I can still see his small, blond self stumble to the stand, punch the ball hard, and fall to the floor.

The ball had rebounded and hit him squarely in the face, giving him a bloody nose for Christmas.

My dad moved toward him, but Mother pushed him aside, pulling tissues from her apron pocket, lifting Danny's head and shouting, "I told you we shouldn't have bought this! But, no, you had to go and buy . . . ."

For one moment, I froze. I couldn't believe what I was hearing.

"*We* shouldn't have bought this . . . ?" She was saying *they* bought it, not Santa? I ran from the room.

Up until Christmas 1947, life had been simple and predictable for me. We'd heard nothing further about Mrs. McCoy, although I recall some discussion about her and mother exchanging letters for awhile. Granny Bill was in my life, so the issue of who was my grandmother was no longer in my mind. But after that Christmas, things seemed more complicated, as if something had loosened my connection to reality.

How could this happen in such a short time? My mother's crying and extracting a promise from me, one that I couldn't share with my father; the possibility of having a wicked stepmother; no Santa Claus.

Secrets.

How was it possible that my father would leave? It had never occurred to me. Things were not as they appeared, nor even as my parents had led me to believe.

I don't remember what I got for Christmas that year.

Mother at 28, 1950

My father (L) and co-worker
1958

1944, Dad and Danny

During Granny's worst days, enduring radium treatment for cancer, she turned The Pioneer over to my mother to manage. Mom immediately took down the beer garden sign and called it a Drive-Inn with modern cabins. She brought in a band on weekends and put white table cloths on the tables in the dance hall, hoping to lure a better crowd from Logan. Unfortunately, the crowd never came up this far on Route 119.

The Parties and the Music

1950, The Pioneer Inn & Beer Garden, Sarah Ann, West Virginia

George Marzetti* was handsome in a way my white-bread family wasn't. He was dark skinned, with thick, black, Bryl-creamed hair that waved ever so slightly on the right side, a skim of shadow even though the heavy smell of lavender told you he'd just shaved. George was my dad's best friend—the kind who got drunk and partied with him on Friday nights, argued politics with him and the other mine supervisors at the Smoke House on Saturday afternoons, and laughed and told stories to entertain my mother and his girlfriend, Betty. Betty worked part-time as a waitress at the Pioneer, so George became a regular customer as well. He and my dad loved to talk Logan County politics, what good friends they were and how George could talk his way out of any mess. Both agreed about one thing.

"Friends are better than family anytime, by god! And don't you forget it."

In the early 1950's, when I was about ten, we were back living upstairs above the Pioneer Beer Garden. If the Pioneer were crowded, the foursome would party upstairs over the beer garden on Friday nights, with the wrap-around windows open to the darkness, the green neon sign above the bar, and the occasional passing car. Otherwise, they'd party in the dance hall, late at night when most of the patrons had gone.

My dad was a fun drunk when he was young, in his early 30's. He loved music and he encouraged me to sing along with the pop tunes of the day, as well as appreciate arias from familiar operas. We loved all kinds of music, enjoying country and western and even Mantovani. Once, when I was playing up in the hills behind the house at dinnertime, he dragged the Victrola out to the back porch, put on a Puccini opera and turned it up loud so I could hear it. My heart, already filled with the orange and golds of autumn leaves and the deep familiar smell of earth, overflowed to hear such beautiful music, and I raced down the hill towards home.

It was a beautiful way he had of reaching me.

Dad was a good dancer, and people always remarked how he looked just like Fred Astaire. He even had developed a soft shoe routine that he'd show off to anyone willing to watch. I might never have overcome my shyness about dancing if he hadn't taken an interest. I could hardly walk through the dance hall without him grabbing my arm. I'd stand on his feet and we'd twirl around the room. We'd practice the box-step waltz, with him showing me all kinds of variations on the step. We even did the tango when the song *Blue Tango* was popular. He loved to jitterbug, but I was just too clumsy and tried his patience, so he'd attempt to drag my mother onto the floor. She was okay as a dancer, but he was eloquent.

My favorite dance of all times was the polka. We nearly wore out the juke box version of *Beer Barrel Polka*, playing it over and over, moving quickly around the outer perimeters of the beer-infested dance floor, until he'd be out of breath and could hardly stand up.

"You're killing me," he would say, and throw himself across the old Wurlitzer, as if to stop the music.

George liked to dance, too, but I didn't like dancing with him. There was something unnerving about the way he'd hold me, and I'd just stiffen up and lose my step. All in all, they were pretty decent drunks, my dad and George—which is to say, they never got into fights with each other.

The two of them usually started drinking in the kitchen while my mother and Betty would get "made up" for their Friday evening. My mother perched in front of the maple dresser, pulling on her nylon stockings, carefully adjusting the seams, blotting the blue-red lipstick on toilet paper, tucking stray ends of auburn hair with black hair pins. Laughing and gossiping, she took her time deciding what jewelry to wear, holding up various earrings, turning her head this way and that, while Betty, using the Maybelline brush, gave careful attention to her dark eyebrows. I'd lie on the bed watching them and listening to their stories and the clinking of ice in their glasses; the combined smell of Seagrams 7, Tabu Perfume and cigarette smoke filling my imagination about what it meant to be a grown-up woman.

By the time my mother and Betty joined the men, the Seagrams and 7 Up had worked its magic. If their Friday night party was upstairs, they'd pull the Victrola into the glassed-in living room, get out the 78's and move the furniture back against the one wall. George and Betty were so glad to have some private time, away from George's wife, they'd be draped around each other, half dancing to

Vaughn Monroe, while my dad would try to persuade my mother to dance or he'd just sing along and soft-shoe with the Mills Brothers.

After a couple more drinks, my mother, who always needed to be the center of attention, would get a little loud, and she was never too embarrassed in front of George or Betty to accost my father with various complaints of the day. Sometimes it was the run-of-the-mill "you never" variety.

"You never wipe your feet and I'm always cleaning up after you." Or, "You never did go visit my mother when she was sick."

But there were many times when Friday night fights got more serious.

"You never take me anywhere! You and George, always running around together. What's the matter, ain't I good enough to be seen with you?"

Her tone of voice was sharp and mean but never shrill, and my father would try to soothe her with stone denial.

"Aw, Melba, you know that's not true."

It seldom worked. George would try to distract her—and protect my dad—by telling a joke or by trying to get her to sing one of her favorite songs. If he succeeded, we were all lucky, because hell raisin' was her forte.

Mother had an untrained but beautiful, husky voice and could sometimes be flattered into an *a cappella* version of one of her favorites.

See the pyramids along the Nile. Watch the sun rise on a tropic isle . . . . You belong to me.

Or she might even do a Charleston to the ever-favorite oldie, *If you knew Suzy like I know Suzy. Oh, oh, oh, what a gal!*

Temperamental and insecure, rail thin, beautiful and fragile, she was the lightning rod around which everything revolved in our house.

As their Friday night parties wore on, my brother and I'd be sent to bed, but there was no escaping the music. The drunker they got, the louder the Victrola and the louder their voices. From my bedroom, I also could hear the music from the dance hall downstairs. I'd lie in bed watching the occasional headlight strike the limestone cutaways and hear both *Dance, Ballerina, Dance* from the living room and, from downstairs, Lefty Frizzell singing.

I love you sooo much, it hurts me . . . Darlin' that's why I'm so blue. I'm afraid to go to sleep at night, Afraid of losing you.

Half asleep, I'd wonder about the customers downstairs and who might be playing the jukebox. Was it that sailor from Omar, in full uniform, home on leave, who told me all about his travels around the world? Was he sitting on the bar stool playing those songs for me?

One night, long after I'd fallen off to sleep, my father woke me, dragged off the covers, and told me to get up, that my favorite opera singer, Caruso himself, was downstairs and had come just to sing for me. I rolled over and mumbled something about leaving me alone, knowing they were all really drunk by now and I didn't want to be part of whatever it was that was going on. Not to be deterred, and counting on my love of Caruso, my father picked me up, carried me downstairs and put me on the lap of a heavy, slightly tipsy stranger sitting near the coal stove in the dance hall.

In my pajamas, rubbing the sleep from my eyes, I squirmed uneasily, looking around the room to see what was going on. Then the stranger began to sing, and for a few moments, I was transported. I thought it *was* Caruso come back from the dead. I was as thrilled as

I was scared, feeling the rise and fall of his large chest, and hearing live, in person, someone singing *Vesti La Giubba* from *Pagliacci.* I knew the aria from the scratchy album my dad and I sometimes listened to, and here was this stranger singing it just for me.

I must have fallen asleep in his arms, as the next thing I knew it was morning, and I was lying there in my bed trying to piece together the events of the night before, trying to separate dreams from reality.

West Virginia Politics

1951, The Pioneer Inn & Beer Garden, Sarah Ann, West Virginia

Granny Bill used to say, "They ain't no dirtier politics than what you get in Logan County."

I can see her shaking her head, hands on her ample hips and tsk, tsking into her luxurious bosom, "Ain't no dirtier politics than Logan County, West, by god, Virginia anywhere in this country."

She knew what she was talking about. She'd been paying off successive county sheriffs and judges for years. It wasn't an uncommon practice in Logan County, although I didn't know this until much later. The sheriff would send a "notifier" up Route 119 to the Pioneer to warn her she was about to be busted by the law.

As often as not, the notice came from one of the Blankenship* boys, who'd walk the half mile to tell her, "We got a phone call from the sheriff's office, Aunt Billie; he's sending some men up here tonight."

The Blankenships had the last phone up our way at the time and, even though we weren't related, they, like most people, called my grandmother Aunt Billie.

In the 1950's, Granny had a license to sell 3.2% beer at the Pioneer but no license for the hard stuff that was passed in the back kitchen or at the end of the counter in front. West Virginia was still a dry state; you had to go to the ABC, or Alcoholic Beverage Control Store, in Logan, 15 miles away, during daytime hours to purchase any beer over 3.2%. If it was whiskey you wanted, you had to buy the whole bottle from the ABC man.

A few hours after Granny was notified, a couple of deputized, dried-up, old coal miners on relief would show up, with papers saying they had a right to search. She usually, but not always, had enough forewarning to hide the hard stuff in one of the cinder-block motel cabins out back.

Only once do I remember her being busted without notice. It was in 1948 and I was seven years old. My parents, brother, and I were living upstairs over the Pioneer, due to the mines being closed down and all. On the night in question, I woke up to gunshots just below my bedroom window. There was Granny Bill, aiming her pistol at some stranger's feet. He was drunk and lumbering around between the silver maple *allee*, saying, "Now Billie, it's not my fault. The sheriff said 'git up there an' take care of that damn situation.'"

Both terrified and fascinated by the scene below, I stood in the dark window, pulling the blanket tighter around my shoulders. I could tell she wasn't trying to hurt the man, just scare the devil out of him.

"I paid my money ever' month," she shouted, "and he sends some drunk up here to mess with me and no warning? You tell that som'bitch to come up here hisself."

"Now, Billie, I caint be . . ."

Pow! Pow! Pow!

I watched her chase him down the blacktop road, shooting into the air; saw him slide down the bushy ridge toward the bridge that led over to Hatfield land. I could see the overgrown hillside brush move out of the shadows cast by a passing car and the neon lights, as he stumbled towards safety. She crossed back over the road toward the lights of the Pioneer, whistling and swinging the pistol by her side, house slippers flip flopping against the dry tarmack road.

I remember smiling and thinking, "Nobody messes with my granny!" as I climbed back in bed.

The next day I heard someone say the man had passed out and spent the night alongside the creek—the creek where we swam in summer and got baptized before winter.

By the early 1950's, however, Granny was well situated with the sheriff's office. With a car trunk full of half-pints and a little vote hauling, she had made sure George Marzetti got elected. He owed her so big, he wouldn't dare bust her business. And what he owed her most for was her silence.

Always figured as a ladies' man, George had finally stepped over the line. He fell into Granny's bad graces when he got Betty pregnant and wouldn't divorce his wife. Granny got in his face and told him off but then kept quiet, kept Betty on the payroll, and played midwife when Betty's time came.

I couldn't have been more than twelve when Betty delivered her baby. We'd gone to Granny's farm in Virginia for some reason, and there being no doctor around for miles, Granny and Mom were expected to do the job. I watched them prepare the bedroom off the kitchen, putting a large rubber pad under several layers of sheets, and tying the ends of one sheet to the bed posts.

"That's for Betty to pull on," I heard Granny say.

I had a hard time figuring out how all this was supposed to happen and certainly couldn't imagine a baby coming through the hole where I peed. That's what I thought at the time.

I helped by carrying buckets of water up from the springhouse and hoisting them up on the wood stove so there'd be plenty of boiling water to keep things sterile, as Mom said. Granny gave me two old sheets and told me to tear them into big rags, just in case she needed them. Betty was screaming and yelling and crying as she got into the bed.

Mom told me to stay in the kitchen and keep the fire going. I stayed in the kitchen, but near the door, so I could see what was going on. More blood, more pushing and screaming than I'd ever seen, and, suddenly, Granny handed me a naked baby girl, all blue and crying, and told me to "clean her up!"

They hadn't prepared me for this. All I knew to do was wrap her in one of the big rags, put her down on the kitchen table, near the stove, wet the other rags in the warm water and wipe her down. Then I wrapped her in a warm towel and sat near the stove, rocking her, staring down at this blue baby who had been covered with blood and stringy mucus, now screaming at the top of her lungs.

I was praying she'd turn the right color soon, because I couldn't imagine otherwise.

Betty finally settled down to whimpering, and Granny kept saying she'd done good, everything was all right. Mom was rushing about with bloody sheets but stopped to look at the newborn.

"Isn't she pretty," she said.

No, I thought. She's not pretty at all; why are you lying?

Granny yelled for me to bring in the baby, and I was glad to see everyone smile at this strange creature I laid in Betty's arms.

"She don't have all her oxygen up yet," Granny cooed to the baby.

"She's got strong lungs, so she'll be fine, just fine, soon enough."

A couple of weeks later, Granny announced she'd found a proper home for the new baby girl they'd named Linda. I kept asking why we couldn't keep it, and she simply said, "Not possible!"

I often wonder if the child knows of her origins. Would it be important to her, the way it was to my mom? How does a mother feel when giving away her child? What does it do to the child?

In the end, Granny found a good home for the baby, never told George's wife, and got Betty some money out of the deal. Later on, Betty left West Virginia and married someone named Jack. I don't know if she had any other children.

Yes, Granny had the goods on Sheriff Marzetti for life. For that matter, she had the goods on a lot of folks in Logan County.

Stuckey and the Bus

Early Summer, 1952, Sarah Ann, West Virginia

The first time I hid on Stuckey's bus, I was about eleven. I'd gotten the idea while sitting on the metal railing of a concrete bridge—the one that led from Granny's place to the large bottom she'd purchased from the Hatfields.

Sitting on the railing, doing nothing on this particular day, I listened to the sounds of the rocky creek below and watched the crows circling the narrow road that cut through the steep mountains ahead. That road was the only way in or out of Sarah Ann, where we lived then. Wearing my cut-off shorts and tee shirt, I was bored, killing time, skipping stones across the narrow, burping creek.

A Trailways bus approached the bend in the road, coming from across the mountain with folks from Williamson and Harlan, and, as it went by, several passengers turned to look out the window at me, doing nothing.

As the Trailways went by, I suddenly saw myself on that bus, looking out at the world, not just being seen. Immediately, a plan formed in my head—a plan that involved the local bus line and Stuckey the driver.

Three times a day, Stuckey drove the local bus up Route 119 through the coal mining towns of Switzer and Omar and turned around outside Granny's place. The Pioneer was the end of the line for the local bus, and Stuckey always took a short break for coffee and gossip with the locals—who were usually drinking beer at the bar, no matter the time of day.

On a day when he was fully engaged in conversation, I saw my chance. I slipped out Granny's back door and went around the front side of the parked vehicle, not wanting to be seen. The door of the bus was open to let in any breeze, and I scrunched down between seats in the back, sweating from the summer heat and the fear of being caught. I waited quite a few minutes before Stuckey came out—him never thinking to look in the back of the bus.

He turned the key and moved onto the road. After a while—just long enough so it'd be difficult for him to stop, put me off, and tell me to "git on home"—I stood up and walked casually down the aisle toward the front, hands tapping the backs of the seats as I moved. The large rear view mirror reflected the shock on his wide, sunburned face when he saw me, and he started to brake but had no shoulder to pull over on.

"What the hell," he gasped, as his face turned redder and perspiration settled above his upper lip.

"What are you doing here, child?"

"Nothing. I just wanted to go to town."

"How did you get on? I didn't see you." He wiped his face on his sleeve and bent down to look me in the eye through the rear view mirror, as if he weren't sure I was actually there, on *his* bus.

"You were inside, "I shrugged. "I just snuck on."

"Your grandmother is going to kill you . . . and me!"

He nodded for me to sit down as we rounded another curve.

I stumbled onto the front seat, from which I could see everything, and, for several minutes, Stuckey said nothing. He'd just look over, shake his head, and look back at the road again. I could see people going about their daily lives: hanging laundry, working on cars, rocking babies on front porches. They passed quickly in front of my eyes, giving me a strange feeling of being there but not there.

So this was what travelling was like!

Stuckey drove six or eight miles to Switzer before stopping at Andy and Stella's grocery store to call Granny and tell her of my whereabouts. I stayed on the bus and wondered how the conversation was going. I also didn't want to explain myself to Granny's sister, Stella.

When Stuckey came out, he handed me a soda pop and said, "You're gonna get it when you get home, young lady."

"I don't care," I replied carelessly, enjoying the sting of the Coca Cola and feeling quite sure of myself. Where did this confidence come from? I didn't think Granny would be too mad. She might even be proud of me. I was like her. I got up and did things I wanted to do.

From up high on the bus, familiar sites took on a different perspective. From where I sat, everything looked smaller, almost like those little villages my friends' mothers would put on the mantles at Christmastime. The porches where school friends and I played during the school year were dusty gray and lifeless in the summer heat. Someone had drawn a big heart with an arrow through it on the soot-covered company store window. The two mannequins were sporting the same outfits they'd worn all summer and both looked tired of it. A group of boys sat along the railroad tracks, smoking and flicking cigarette butts. A hunched-over, old man swept the dirt in front of the tiny post office. I opened the window next to me and stuck my head out, loving the breeze that whipped my face and turned my sweaty hair into wild curls.

I was going somewhere! By myself!

I didn't hear the three o'clock whistle as we passed the coal tipple because Stuckey was hitting the horn and waving to the men leaving work.

"Hey, how're you doing?"

White eyes and pink mouths emerged from black, coal-dusted faces as they returned his greeting. The men, who had worked the six a.m. to three p.m. shift, all looked the same to me, just like my dad when he came home from the mines and headed to the basement to shower. Mom wouldn't let him in the house until he had cleaned himself up downstairs.

What is it like, I wondered, to work down in the mines? Do these men recognize each other underneath that black dust? What do they talk about? Do they crawl on their bellies like my dad told me? And what was this thing about not allowing women to go beyond the face of the mine? Some kind of superstition, I'd heard.

Stuckey and I didn't talk much; he had the radio going. The music was high lonesome—Hank Williams' songs I was familiar with from Granny's juke box—and Stuckey hummed along, turning from time to time to look at me and shake his head. He did ask about school and I told him it was good; I liked it. I played with the straw in my Coke, tying it in knots as I looked around, hoping to see someone I knew and could wave to. It occurred to me the high wires along the electric poles from Chauncey to Micco, from Switzer to Monaville were like threads I could follow if I ever got lost.

We passed a tipple that had been shut down. Nobody there. Just slate, ash and smoke on one side, with empty, run-down houses across the road.

"Blow the horn when we go under the train bridge," I told him. "I like that sound."

He held down the horn until we came out the other side, shifting his shoulders from side to side and yelling, "Whoooo, whooo!"

I stomped my feet and we both laughed.

No one flagged the bus on the whole trip to town.

Once in Logan, Stuckey pulled the bus into the station that stood across from the electric company. He parked without effort alongside the other buses, took the metal box from the meter, and told me to come inside. While he turned in his fares and chatted with other drivers, I sat on a stool, twirling around behind the counter where people bought tickets, watching them come and go, and taking small bites of the tootsie roll one of the drivers had given me. From time to time, the other drivers looked my way and tipped their caps.

The man at the counter asked if I knew how to make change. I nodded eagerly.

"I help my granny out in her business all the time."

"Anybody buying a ticket for West Hamlin—that's the next bus out—tell 'em it's $1.15 and give 'em change. You know how to do that?"

"Yes, sir."

"I'll be right back. Any problems, tell 'em to wait."

Only one customer came to the window while he was gone; she wanted to cash a money order, so I told her she'd have to wait for the dispatcher. Meanwhile, I wondered about ordering money and how that worked.

After a half hour or so, Stuckey told me to, "Get on a stick," and I hurried to the Whites Only rest room to pee before the trip home.

He had me board ahead of the other passengers so I could get the front seat and he could keep an eye on me. A few people, none of whom I knew, got on—one, a young girl with a crying baby, went all the way to the back and sat by herself, jiggling the baby up and down and staring out the window. An old couple sat together and I noticed the man carried a tin can which he spat into from time to time. A sleepy high school boy slouched down, pulled his cap over his eyes, crossed his arms, and, apparently, fell asleep.

The trip to Sarah Ann went quickly. Nobody talked; the baby stopped crying. The old couple pulled the cord and got off in lower Switzer; the girl and baby, in Omar; and, just as we rounded the curve in Crystal Block, the sleepy boy yelled, "Stop here."

Stuckey slowed to a stop on the nearest shoulder, and the boy jumped off the top step, almost falling into a ditch covered with mulberry bushes and stray purple wildflowers.

"Are you nervous?" Stuckey asked, as we neared the Pioneer. "Your granny's going to whip your butt."

"No, she won't," I held out. "She knows I like to travel."

As I look back at those days, I still feel the excitement of going somewhere on my own, not asking for permission, feeling bold and courageous. Just like the time before my second husband and I divorced. I wanted to escape the winter and the fear and confusion of that time. Without consulting anyone, I booked a trip to Mexico, all on my own. This required the same kind of forced confidence I needed to get on Stuckey's bus, and I was rewarded with a new sense of confidence, knowing I had the ability to survive on my own.

Even in a strange place. I would do fine by myself.

Granny's farm in Meadow View, Va, on the
outskirts of Abingdon.

Summers on the Farm

1953, in Sarah Ann, West Virginia and at Granny's farm outside
Abingdon, Virginia

"Let's us go wash the cabin windows today," Granny Bill said on a Saturday morning, just before school let out.

Always glad to be with her, whatever the situation, I agreed to just about anything she suggested. To the side of the beer garden was a long, cinderblock building, containing eight cabins with shared bathrooms. Granny had them built alongside The Pioneer in the 1930's, as she saw the opportunity for housing and boarding Works Progress Administration (WPA) road construction workers. By the late 1940's, the WPA construction had ended, and most rooms were rented for half-days or by the hour.

"Get that pan from under the sink while I look for some rags," Granny began on that warm Saturday morning. "Now fill that with water—not too hot, not too cold. Get you the vinegar from the pantry and pour about a cup in there and mix it around. That's good.

Now you take that pan out to the first cabin, and come on back here to help me with the ladder."

I walked carefully with the pan while she yelled after me, "Don't look at the water, you'll only spill it! Just look ahead to where you're going."

After putting down the pan on the sidewalk, I skipped back into the kitchen to find her tearing old sheets into rags.

"There's a little ladder out in the shed; go find that one. And hurry up."

The shed had one side filled with coal and the other with everything we didn't throw out or drag over to the creek bank. Things somebody might need someday. She knew I could easily be distracted by the old mirrors, the busted cupboards and rusty machine parts, boxes of canning jars and empty beer bottles.

Make-believe came easy to me. If I weren't fast enough, she'd come after me.

"You know, if I was to fall sick, I'd probably die before you could get me to the doctor. Hurry up, slow poke."

The six-foot wooden ladder wasn't just heavy, it was awkward for me, a twelve year old, to carry. She'd help by offering, "Put it up on your shoulder. That'll balance the weight for you."

Her rough hands full of clean rags, she stood under the maple tree, out of the heat, watching me struggle to put down the ladder and set it up against the window.

"Not *on* the window, silly. Put it up against the frame so you don't break the glass. Good! You got it. Now take this here rag—wring it out some—and climb up there and wipe those top windows."

The smell of the cider vinegar in the water and the chickory and dandelions underneath the windows all combined to give me a feeling of security and familiarity. Granny Bill offered up a dry rag and then rinsed the wet one for the next set of panes. After I'd washed four or five sets of windows, she'd throw the water over the chickory and dandelions—"Best way to kill these weeds," she say, handing me the pan and telling me to, "Go get some more."

This would go on until the sixteen windows fronting the eight motel cabins were sparkling and the yellow dandelions were drooping in the hot sun.

Over the years, I learned that when she said, "Let's us do something," it meant there was something she wanted done and she wanted someone else to do it while she supervised.

"Let's us clean the kitchen" meant I'd end up doing the dishes and sweeping the floor. She'd offer encouragement with, "Don't forget that corner now," or, "Be sure you sweep under the table."

"Let's us take this trash out" meant I was expected to do the job. This communication became known throughout the family as a *Billie Brown Job*. People would start walking the minute they heard, "Let's us . . ."

Each summer until I was thirteen, Granny would gather my brother and me and one or two cousins, and drive us from West Virginia to her farm outside Abingdon, Virginia. We'd spend the summers helping Granny on the farm, giving the adults a break from our summer energy and me a chance to be with my grandmother full-time.

She would load us all into her maroon Kaiser with the radio and soft leather seats, giving each of us a brown bag to put under our shirts, saying, "This will keep you from getting sick." It was only years later that I wised up to the real use for the bags. There would be no throwing up on the seats of her car!

As she drove the snakelike curves through the West Virginia mountains and into the valleys of the Blue Ridge, Granny would sing along with the radio—songs like, *You are my sunshine, my only sunshine,* and the one I loved, *If I had the wings of an angel, over these prison walls I would fly.*

She'd also point out various historic sites along the four-hour drive.

"Over there's where that boy killed a mountain lion with his own hands. They hung it on that road sign there so folks could see it."

Important, *historic* information, she'd say, making me laugh at her serious tone and her teasing us.

"This here's where poor Charlie drove over the hill two years ago. He and Lena was drinking and took this curve too fast. They's lucky to be alive." A true story, but *historic?*

Her brother, Charlie, was always referred to as *poor Charlie,* as he could be one lazy son-of-a-gun. It was said that he once applied for a job at the mines when coal was in demand and jobs were widely available. He was turned down when he said, "Ya'll don't have any work for me, do you?"

Granny's stories about *history* and relatives were always more interesting than what I ever found in my books.

We did make some actual historic trips after she started getting radium treatments for cancer and seeing the cancer doctor at the University of Virginia Hospital in Charlottesville. She'd sometimes take me, my brother, and our older cousin, Curtis, with her, and we stopped to visit Thomas Jefferson's Monticello home on the way. We'd wander the rooms and she'd remind us to pay attention to what great men could accomplish. Monticello was the most beautiful place I'd ever seen, and I was fascinated with the weighted clock and dumb waiter Jefferson had invented.

Bathroom breaks on our summer trip to the farm were planned for the halfway mark. "Let's stop up here on top of the mountain and take in the view. You kids go over in the bushes there and hurry up. We're not stopping again."

We'd do our business, admire the view for a minute or two, and climb back in the car. To keep down the backseat noise and fighting, she'd create games: who could count the most cows in the next ten miles; who could recognize the most out-of-state license plates; who could sing all the words of a particular song; who could do their six's and seven's?

Sometimes she'd reach under her seat and pull out a bag of chips or Cheez-Its and toss it into the back seat, warning, "If you kids don't shut up, I'm going to put somebody out on the road and you'll be sorry."

That warning would quiet us down for awhile, as we'd all heard the story of how she actually did that to my mom when she was little.

Once we'd turned off the highway onto the road that led to the farm, the pavement disappeared and the path narrowed. I'd hang out the windows to grab at the huckleberry bushes and stick dogwoods, while Granny would toot the car horn to let neighboring farmers know we'd arrived.

In the car, she had explained all the jobs that would be required of us over the summer. We knew we were expected to work hard, and there'd be hell to pay if we were caught sneaking off or shirking our responsibilities.

It was such a relief to be away from my parents' arguing. For the most part, I never minded the work on the farm. I loved the summers, where I could play and daydream and be responsible and needed at the same time. In between various jobs, I'd wander the apple orchard between Granny's farm and that of Charlie and Lena and lie in the field, studying cloud formations, wondering what was out there beyond the clouds.

The smell and taste of fresh green apples outdid any dessert I could think of, but too many caused a heap of stomach trouble. The scent of sweet clover followed me up into the out-buildings, where we stored farm equipment, hung tobacco to dry, or smoked hams. I could hide and look through spaces between the old logs at whatever was going on around me.

Up until I was twelve, I had a special project that I loved to work on each summer. In earlier visits to Granny's farm, I started building cities and roadways out of the red clay mud under the front porch and along the cow path near the corn silo. Each summer, I'd add new buildings or plant small trees and flowers. Eventually, Granny said I was too old for such stuff, and I reluctantly gave it up.

What I loved most about those summers is that I could go with my grandmother on her errands to Abingdon or Damascus and keep her company while she visited neighbors. We'd sit on neighbors' porch steps and discuss the weather and crops and find out about people's health. We never went to Abingdon without stopping at the thrift shop, as Granny always knew some family who'd just had a new baby or whose kids needed new shoes or school clothes. She made sure people had what they needed.

My main work for the summers was to feed the chickens, gather the eggs, help with the cooking, do the dishes, work the wringer washing machine, bring up water from the spring down the hill, and help with a few field jobs.

I complained only when I had to carry the buckets of water up the hill from the spring. My sides hurt. My cousin, Curtis, complained that I was only trying to get out of work, but Granny would tell my brother or someone older to meet me halfway and bring the buckets the rest of the way up the steep slope. Even though I was expected to work hard, like everyone else, I always knew she watched out for me.

When I was twelve and got my period, along with bad cramps, she'd make the boys do my work that day and she'd give me a big spoonful of paregoric and let me sleep on her bed.

Curtis was my older cousin by seven years. His mother, Tootsie, Granny's younger sister, had epileptic seizures and died when the cigarette she was smoking fell onto her dress during a seizure. There was no way Curtis' father, Roscoe, could care for three boys, ages nine, fourteen and sixteen at the time, so they were parceled out among the family. The oldest, Charles Ray, finished high school quickly enough and went into the Army. We had a framed picture of him in his uniform on top of the television in the living room.

In 1953, Granny had the first television out in the country, and, on weekends she'd sometimes invite neighboring farmers to come over and watch wrestling or Jackie Gleason. We'd turn off all the lights; adults would crowd onto the couch and chairs, children on the floor, and we'd stare, mesmerized by the black and white figures moving and talking in front of us.

We were not allowed to talk when the television was on.

Granny had taken in Curtis and his younger brother, Donald, but couldn't handle both boys *and* the farm *and* her beer garden in West Virginia and all the other family concerns. Donald appeared to suffer the most from his mother's death and needed lots of attention;

he stopped eating and talking and couldn't walk. His Uncle Roosevelt carried him around and force fed him for months. Ultimately, he went to live with Aunt Stella before she and Andy set up a business in Logan County. Just a quarter mile down the road from Granny's farm, Donald was always part of the extended summer family.

On the farm, Curtis was expected to *be the man around the house*—there being no husband in Granny's life at this time—and he inherited the hardest of labor; at fifteen he was plowing the fields with the old tractor, fixing it when it broke down, cutting and hanging the tobacco, milking the cows, maintaining the pile of firewood, and keeping the fires going on cold nights. In general, he did whatever needed to be done. In return, Granny gave him room and board, clothes, shoes, and books for school. She taught him to drive her Kaiser and, unfortunately for him, offered up a great deal of criticism about how fast he drove, how he braked and parked the car. I learned a lot about driving by listening to her advice to Curtis.

Curtis was born with a crossed eye, and Granny made it her business to find a doctor in Charlottesville who could straighten the eye. Her attitude was, "If you can fix something, you ought to do it!" She helped her nephews in many ways, but I could see she didn't lather them with affection. Maybe it was just her way of treating boys, for I certainly knew I was special and got hugs to prove it. I think it must have been hard for Curtis and Donald to know they depended on the good graces of family. When Curtis had the chance to supervise Danny and me without Granny around, he was bossy and mean. He'd play tricks on us, like short-sheeting us or putting pine cones in our pillows.

"It's about time for us to plant some more potatoes," Granny said one day, looking up at the sky and sensing rain. "Let's go down and see if Curtis has turned over that part of the field." We walked down the hill to the vegetable garden, on the sunny side of the tobacco barn Roscoe had built, to see if Curtis had plowed and whether the soil was dry enough for planting the potatoes. The conditions seemed right to her, and she sent me back to the house to bring down the burlap bag of seed potatoes she'd put aside in the fall.

"Be careful now, don't bruise them."

The damp, moldy bags were heavy, and, when I knew she couldn't see me, I'd roll the bag down the hill, kicking at it with my Buster Browns, until the bag leveled off just to the shady side of the barn. Then I'd pick it up and haul it to where she'd be standing, studying the field.

"Now here's what we're going to do," she'd say. "You put that potato in the mound, with the cut side down, and cover it up real good and I'll grunt."

"What do you mean, Granny?"

"You bend down, plant the potato, and I'll grunt for you. That's my part."

I knew she was being silly; I also knew she meant it! This was another *Billie Brown Job*; I was to do the work, while she'd stand by to be sure I was doing it right. Even though it may have been burdensome, I always learned from her instructions.

The only job I really hated was weeding the tobacco seedling bed.

The bed itself stretched about 30-feet long by about 10-feet deep alongside the barn. As the seeds took root and began to nudge aside the dry earth, so did the weeds. It was important to pull out the weeds so that the plants could grow strong and tall. When the seedlings were about eight or ten inches tall, they'd be carefully removed and planted in the larger field, which was Granny's acreage allotment for tobacco.

Actually, she had more than her allotment of tobacco growing just past the cornfield, which wasn't legal.

"This way, if the field don't yield a good crop, I can always take a good load to market from my other field."

Always one step ahead.

Weeding the tobacco bed meant working on my hands and knees under the scorching sun, reaching as far as I could from the sides into the bed, being careful not to squash the other seedlings. It was a dreadful, boring, sweaty job and nobody ever volunteered to help. I resented the fact that it was considered a girl's job—meaning I wasn't allowed to drive the tractor. I wasn't good enough at milking the cows. And I certainly wasn't strong enough to cut timber for firewood.

I'd pull a few weeds, then wander over to the spring for cold water, then head back to the bed, sweating and scratching and very unhappy.

One day, from out of nowhere, it occurred to me I didn't have to be stuck with this job. There was a way out. It was dangerous, but I decided to take it.

I looked around and saw Granny heading down the hill to check on me, and I began to pull out everything within my reach: weeds and seedlings alike. I was in a frenzy, knowing what I was in for but accepting my fate.

Sometimes, you just have to break the rules to get what you want, I told myself, assigning little weight to the punishment that was bound to come.

As Granny rounded the barn, she was fanning herself with her apron, saying how hot it was and didn't I want to take a break and get us some water. Her first look at the bare patch of the tobacco bed told me to run for my life. And run, I did.

Down past the driveway to the barn, jumping over cow pies and thistle, over the stream that flowed from the cool, shady spring, out toward the unpaved road that led to neighboring farms and, hopefully, safety, only to be stopped by a rusty gate latch that moved too slowly.

She caught me. Swearing I was the dumbest kid she'd ever met, not to know the difference between weeds and tobacco, she gave me the spanking of my life.

I was never allowed to work the tobacco bed again.

This picture was taken in 1953.
Granny's doctor at the University of Virginia in
Charlottesville had only recently told her she had less than a
year to live. that he'd done all he could. She told him and
others, "Oh, no. I'm too mean to die!" True to her word, she
lived another 25 years, fighting cancer until the end of 1978.

Let's Go in Here and Talk

1952, Granny's Farm

"Let's go in here and talk," she said, guiding my shoulder toward her bedroom. Granny Bill closed the door and sat on the small stool that fronted her oversized maple dresser. She fidgeted with her hand mirror and comb while I looked around, not knowing whether to sit or stand. I settled on the sunny spot on the floor, across from her bed. The three-paneled mirror on the dresser reflected her softness from every side.

"They's some things we have to talk about that ain't easy to talk about. Do you understand?" She bent down to look me in the eye.

I shrugged, "I guess so." I could tell this was going to be a grown-up conversation.

"Now, your daddy's a good man, Janet. Sometimes he don't act like it, but he means well, you understand?"

I nodded, agreeing with her, even though from an early age, I was aware of a strangeness in my parents. They weren't like my friends' parents, what with my mother disappearing every so often and my dad somehow persuading or coercing her back to the family.

We'd adjust, she'd rearrange all the furniture I had placed, and then be off again.

This time, as soon as my dad left for Tampa to work for a friend of his—a necessity while the mines were closed—Mom left in a flash with her cousin, Pauline, headed for West Palm Beach and what they considered the good life—taking jobs as waitresses in a steakhouse. Nobody needing her or telling her what to do.

She left Danny and me behind with Granny, with strict instructions not to say a word to Dad about her whereabouts. I was trying to remember how long she'd been gone when Granny pulled at my shirt.

"Are you listening to me, girl? He's a good man, but his coming in and taking you and Danny out of school today . . . well . . . that wasn't right," she hesitated.

In the silence, I waited, studying a filmy rainbow on the wall and following it to its source, the light bouncing off the metal strip of her pine handkerchief box and spreading across the big pink roses on the wall. I always thought of her bedroom as The Rose Room because of the wallpaper and the roses on the linoleum. Today, the room smelled of Pond's Cold Cream and my own sweat.

Earlier today, my classroom had the smell of sweet lilac. I sat there, with the other sixth graders, trying to pay attention to the geography lesson about North and South America, but I was daydreaming and inhaling the lilacs blooming outside the half-open window.

"There ain't nothing sweeter than lilacs and peonies," Granny would say. Then we'd laugh and exclaim, "Except for you!" and chase each other to give love pinches that always ended in hugs and kisses and giggles.

North and South America got dropped like a hot potato when my father walked into the classroom. His sudden appearance startled even the world map that was pulled down over the black board and it waved him by. He stood at the edge of a row of wooden desks, looking down each one 'til he found me.

"Janet, get your books and come with me."

Mrs. Mercer tried to say something, but he cut her off.

"She won't be back."

My surprise was stung with fear and excitement at seeing him after so many months.

"Somebody must be bad sick, for him to be here," I thought to myself, and hurriedly pulled the books and papers out of my desk, carefully folding my book report down the middle the way Mrs. Mercer liked.

She looked at me questioningly as I handed it to her. My best friend, Phyllis, mouthed, "I'll see you later," and I nodded, not knowing what to expect.

My younger brother, Danny, was waiting in the hallway, trying to balance his books, his Superman lunch box and his baseball bat in thin, 11-year-old arms. He gave me a confused look and I just shrugged.

My mouth tasted like I'd sucked on a piece of metal, and swallowing a lot wasn't helping. My father was quiet on the drive to the farm, saying, "We'll talk about it at home." In the back seat, I hugged my books to my chest as if they would keep me from floating away. Danny sat close, rocking from side to side.

My dad dropped us off by the springhouse, saying, "Go start packing. Tell your granny I'll be right back; I'm going for cigarettes."

Granny cleared her throat, raked her fingers over her knees, and took a deep breath. "What I'm trying to say is, you know how your momma and daddy argue all the time, and your daddy had to go work in Florida when the mines closed down last year?"

The words rushed out before she could call them back. She pulled at the bodice of her house dress and blew air over her large breasts. Nobody ever talked about those arguments between my parents, but here she was, saying the words. I had a spasm of courage and turned to her.

"Well, yes, but nobody ever explained why Mom and Aunt Pauline went to Florida in the first place—the whole other side of the state from where he was. Nobody ever explained that to me." I locked my fingers into a steeple and flushed, fearing my words had sounded harsh.

"Honey, that's what I'm trying to tell you."

"What?"

"Your daddy found out that your mother and Pauline was down there waitressing. Somebody told him; I don't know who. Anyway, he's mad at me for sending your mother's letters to him, the way I did, you know, in that other envelope."

She pulled a handkerchief from her bosom, wiped at a dusting of face powder on the dresser, and then used it to pat her neck dry. She avoided looking at me.

"And?"

The facts were making me dizzy and impatient.

"And, so, he's taking you and Danny away, down to Florida with him. He says you all are leaving tomorrow morning."

She covered her eyes with her hand, as if these words were too much for her.

"I'm sorry, honey; I'm so sorry. You know how your mother can be when she sets her mind to something. I didn't know what else to do."

I knew this letter business had been going on, but nobody ever explained anything. Granny would get a letter from my mother, and there'd be a special envelope in it, addressed to my dad, and Granny would put it out for the mailman. When I'd ask, Granny would just say, "It's for me to know and you to find out, little girl!"

Sometimes there was a letter in the envelope for Danny and me and, sometimes, two crisp one dollar bills. Granny's "*tsk tsking*" at this always made me think she disapproved of children having that much money. It was only later I understood her displeasure with my mother on all fronts.

I sat there, now, knees up against my chest, more confused than ever, inhaling my own smell and trying to cross my toes over one another. I didn't know what to say. I just rocked back and forth and crossed my toes. Granny stood up.

"You're going to have to go with him, honey. He's your daddy. And . . ." she pulled her soft pink dress away from where it had lodged in the crevices of her body, "We have so much to do to get ready! Let's get going, girl!"

As the tears welled up, I opened my eyes wide, trying to stretch my face so they wouldn't fall. It wasn't that I couldn't cry in front of her; I just didn't want to cry over this.

"I'm not going," I coughed. "I'm staying here."

She pulled me to her. "Oh, honey, I'm so sorry. I wish that daughter of mine would grow up. She's hurt you children terribly."

The tears raced down my sunburned face leaving salt lines in their path.

"I'm not going," I said. "I'm staying with you."

"Child, I wish you could. I wish you could. But he's your daddy and he's made up his mind and . . . uh oh, here he is, driving up the hill."

She shook me softly and wiped my face with her handkerchief.

"Go wash up. Don't let him see you this way."

I ran out the back door of the house, past Danny, who was eating crackers and grape jelly on the side porch, further up the hill to a limestone boulder just this side of the top of the hill. I was always happy lying on this rock at night, after dinner and chores were done; studying the stars and wondering about boys and heaven and poems I'd read—all sorts of things—without anxiety, without fear.

I saw my dad walk up on the porch, flick his cigarette away from the house, and go inside. I couldn't tell if he said anything to my brother or not. I stood there against the rock, in the shadow of old cedars, on the edge of the drama about to unfold.

Words escaped me. There were no words to explain all the feelings I had at that moment—hurt and confusion and fear, all bound up with dread. Mostly I was aware of the dread. That unspoken caution about what was to come, a suspicion, waiting for the next shoe to drop, as it, inevitably, would.

How could Granny not stand up for me? Couldn't she see what lay ahead for Danny and me? I needed her and she was stepping back. And here was my father, whom I hadn't seen in months. He was like a stranger, demanding I leave the only place where I felt safe and protected. He wanted to take us from Granny's, where I slept peacefully and woke up to hear her talking about the farm chores of the day and where I knew what was expected of me. Here he was, wanting to take us out of school and away from safety, then drive a thousand miles to confront my mother with her tricks and lies. God knows she was full of them, more than even he suspected.

I thought back to the times when I was about seven and we were living in Omar. She'd wake me in the middle of the night, asking if I'd like an ice cream. No matter what I said, we'd end up at some beer joint down the road. Me, half asleep in my pajamas in a corner booth; her, drinking beer and dancing with some man.

"Now, if your daddy wakes up when we get home, you tell him you wanted an ice cream," she would say.

Right, I thought. Even a second-grader knows that no parent in her right mind would get up and go out in the middle of the night and drive ten or fifteen miles to satisfy a child's desire for ice cream!

And then there was the time she put me to bed in a motel room, while she and her boyfriend took the other bed. I couldn't ignore what I felt at that moment: something bad was going on and there was nothing I could do to stop it.

Why couldn't I fight my mother then? Why didn't I refuse to go along, refuse to be part of her schemes?

Because I was a child? Because another one of those rules said, "Obey your parents, no matter what."? Or because I was, at that time, inescapably bound to her; recognizing that she always won out over my father and my grandmother?

Safety lay in going along, not making waves. None of the grown-ups could deny her; how could I? Her conspiracies trumped the truth every time.

No, I didn't want any part of the arguing and accusations that would fly between them when they met up in West Palm Beach. I'd end up in the middle of their drunken fights. I always did, it seems.

He said . . . she said . . . well, Janet said . . . and Janet knew about it . . . . and, why'd you tell Janet and not me?

Why didn't he just go face her himself, once he found out where she was? Why did he have to drag us along and throw us in her face?

They reminded me of the two black and white terrier dog magnets on glass that were popular in the 1950's, inevitably pulled into each other's magnetic field. There was no escaping each other. I wondered if they knew or even cared how their craziness affected Danny and me, and, just as quickly, answered my own question. "Children are to be seen and not heard." We were irrelevant or, at best, a pawn in their game.

When it came down to it, they were fused like a mobius strip, into one, circular, unbroken connection that could twist into many shapes, but never separate.

I began to wonder if I had the same genes that drove my mother's need for excitement and control, for that adrenaline rush that came with each win, that feeling of being alive. Did I secretly, unconsciously enjoy the excitement, the danger?

I couldn't manage all these thoughts at once, but neither could I hide from the basic and immediate truth.

Having my brother and me in tow gave my father the upper hand. The deck was stacked in his favor this time. One more time, he'd get her back, no matter the cost.

"Oh, god, leave me out of it!" I said out loud, wondering, how could I escape them? Where could I go, if Granny insisted I leave with him? My chest hurt with the knowledge that she wouldn't stand up for me. I didn't like it and yet I understood it.

They were my parents, not her. She had no rights. That had to be the reason; why else would she let me go? That, and the fact that her interference with my mother's will had seldom held fast over the years.

"Your mother's pitiful, Janet," she'd say. "She's sick or she wouldn't be acting this way." As if being sick made it all okay.

The quiet of that dark, star-filled, moonless night, the mist settling over the fields and orchards, brought me to my senses. Reluctantly, exhaling a deep breath, I admitted I had no choice but to go. My back ached from leaning into the cold rock, and I stood to stretch.

"Janet, come help me with dinner." I could see my grandmother calling from the porch. "Come on down, now. We have to eat. Your daddy's hungry."

I walked down to the house. Dad sat at the table with Danny, telling him what to write down on the tablet in front of him. He motioned for me to sit and slid a sheet of lined paper to me.

"I want you to write your mother a letter. Tell her how awful she is for deserting you and Danny. We'll give her the letters when we get there."

Deserted? I didn't feel I'd been deserted. I was happy here.

I protested, "Why are you making us do this? I don't want to write a letter!"

"Sit down and write the letter," he said sternly.

No place to run, no place to hide, I slammed my fist on the table and screamed one last time, "I don't want to go!"

"You're going," he said, his face fiercer than I remembered it, "so sit down and write the damned letter."

Granny busied herself at the stove, stirring the gravy, looking over and shaking her head.

I don't know what I wrote. I pushed down my feelings to hide my helplessness.

"These two are crazy," I thought, as I tore into the lined paper. "How can I trust them?" Somewhere inside myself, I knew I could never totally trust either of them again. I was on my own.

Making It Work

Spring, 1953, From Granny's Farm to Florida

Early the next morning we loaded the car for West Palm Beach. No tears, this time; just quiet resolution on my part. A quick hug for my grandmother, lest I be reconnected to the false hope that I might stay. She must have felt it, for she held my face for a moment and told me to call her if I ever needed her.

"Okay," I said lightly, climbing into the back seat with my pillow, leaving the front for Danny, who seemed to have warmer feelings for my dad than I did at that moment. I didn't wave goodbye or look back.

Much of the trip down Route 1 has faded in my memory, but I did note in my pink, sequin-covered diary that I could add South Carolina, Georgia and Florida to my goal of visiting all 48 states.

A total of seven now; only forty one to go.

I came to life when we stopped in Saint Augustine, the oldest city in the United States, according to my dad.

"Ponce de Leon discovered Florida in the 1500's, and he found the Fountain of Youth here," my dad said, as he slowed the car to point out the trees with hanging moss and the public fountains.

I wasn't at all interested in staying young, nor was I interested in his history lesson. I was gazing at the romantic, old Spanish architecture and the enormous castle and fort, which I also described in my diary later on. Finally, we saw the Atlantic Ocean. Dad pulled into a public parking lot, bought us Cokes and chips and told us we could wade in the surf for a bit.

I stood there, the ocean throwing waves at my stiff, restless legs, and wondered what lay beyond the horizon. The water tasted salty and sweet at the same time. I waded further in, against my father's warnings, planted my feet in the sand, and steadied myself against the undertow threatening to pull me off shore. What would it be like being pulled further out from where I'm standing, I wondered. Where would I end up? Could I float all the way to other countries, other happier worlds?

Danny's splashing brought me back, and Dad's wave signaled it was time to move on.

Over the next several hours, I napped and caught occasional glances of the ocean. The car's abrupt stop woke me. In the darkness, we had pulled up in front of a small bungalow framed with overgrown orange flowers. I grimaced as Dad collected our letters from the glove compartment. He told us to wait in the car, he'd be back shortly.

I was trying to imagine my mother living here and what was going on inside. I rolled down the car window and heard music and my mother's laughter coming from the house. Soon enough the laughter turned to shouting and, before I could prepare myself, my mother was running toward the car, screaming and crying ferociously.

"How could you write such awful things to me? I'm your mother!"

She pulled us from the car, holding me so close, I felt suffocated.

"I knew this would happen," I thought. "Now it's our fault!"

There was no use trying to explain; she'd see it as opposition and get more hysterical, and, anyway, she and Dad were already shouting at each other.

The confrontation between my mother and father was more intense than usual because my father drew the line; she could stay where she was, but he was taking the kids with him to Tampa.

She protested with hysterical cries, "But I'm their mother!" knowing he now had the upper hand.

Not much was required of Danny and me while they argued, so I pretended to be asleep on the couch in the next room, hating that I was put in this situation. They drank and talked and argued into the night.

She chose to stay.

So, just after we ate our baloney sandwiches the next day, the three of us headed west on the two-lane highway that connected to what my dad called, *Alligator Alley*.

We stopped twice; once beside a roadside teepee where dark-faced, square-jawed men dressed like cowboys were selling key chains, dolls and totem poles. It was scary to me but Dad encouraged us to go inside, saying "You may never see a teepee again in this lifetime."

Once inside the teepee, I saw an ancient-looking, wrinkled, old man and woman sitting in the center, colorful blankets around them. They did not move a muscle or recognize our presence in any way. It made me uncomfortable, as if we were watching them live their life as they sat by the side of the road, having people come in and out of their living room; us paying money to stare at them.

I wondered if they liked living like this. Weren't they embarrassed?

It reminded me of how I felt both in and outside my own life. I was glad to leave.

The second stop was at a Stuckey's, which, I discovered, was one big, shiny, happy diner. We'd passed several on the way from Virginia to Florida, but my dad never wanted to stop.

"Them's chain stores," he kept saying, leading my brother and me into an argument as to whether they sold only chains.

As we passed them on Highway 1, I'd note that, "People are carrying food out of there, Daddy . . ." and he'd mumble, "Chain stores," as if they were part of the penitentiary system.

I'd never seen so much stainless steel in my life, except on Aunt Pauline's 1951 Packard. After a stop in the bathroom, Dad said we could each have a Stuckey candy—a caramel log roll covered with pecans and enough sugar to stop your heart. My father drank his coffee with milk and sugar at the counter, while I whirled around on the counter stool, chewing slowly on the candy, trying to imagine where all these people had come from and where they were going.

It seemed everyone was smiling and talking to each other. I could've sat there all day, loving the sweetness and strange friendliness of that place. I thought everyone must be happy to be travelling.

In short order, we were back in the car, me taking the front seat this time. Within the hour, Dad was pointing out the skyline in the distance.

"That's Tampa," he said, adjusting the rear view mirror and sitting up straighter.

"You're going to be living in the big city now. You'll probably have to take buses to school—not school buses, regular buses for people going to business." I half listened to him.

"It's going to be different from being out in the country, but once we get you settled, I think you'll like it here."

All I could think about was how I would fit in at school. Back in Virginia, everyone knew everyone else, no matter what grade you were in. Some of the sixth graders were actually in the same classroom with the seventh graders; classes being so small and all.

Would I be in a big class? Would I have the right clothes for a city school? Would they talk funny?

Danny was asleep in the back seat, wet with sweat and the setting sun beating down on him. I stuck my head out the window and drew back quickly.

"What is that?" I frowned.

Dad laughed and said that was the smell from the soap factory.

"Sometimes it blows our way, but not very often. It's the worst out here."

"I thought soap smelled pretty, like flowers."

"When they finish with it, it does. But they start out with whale blubber and dead fish."

"They do not," I stared at him, knowing he had the teaser in him.

He just laughed and blew his cigarette smoke at me.

"I sure don't want to live with that smell."

He smiled at me and said, "You won't, honey. You won't."

We were all feeling a little easier, having the confrontation and hysterics behind us.

After a minute or two, Dad asked if Granny had had that talk with me.

"What talk?" I was still angry about being pulled away from Granny, and wanted to be stubborn and make him pay for information.

"You know, that girl stuff."

He refocused on the traffic that was accumulating all around us.

"You mean like when girls get their periods and all?"

"No, I don't mean that." He shot me an *Are you stupid*? look and continued.

"I mean about making dinner for Danny and me and doing the washing and ironing."

"What's Danny going to do?"

"Don't start with me, young lady. You know what I'm talking about."

"I'm only twelve almost thirteen years old. I don't know how to do those things."

"Yes, you do. You've helped your mother and your granny enough to have learned something."

I rolled up the window, feeling nauseous from the stench and what lay ahead.

Granny had made it clear I'd have to cook for all of us.

"You're almost thirteen and you been around folks cooking for ages. You can put on a pot of beans, fry some potatoes." And do the laundry.

"People will judge you by the way you hang the laundry," Granny Bill said, as she showed me how to hang the pants from the waist and the shirts by the side seams. "Hang all the shirts together and all the other things together in groups. That shows you know what you're doing," she had said.

What she didn't tell me was how to wash clothes and linens without a washing machine, but I discovered the bathtub was as good as the old washtub we used in the country.

My dad had been living in a small, second-floor, garage apartment, at the end of a short driveway, just behind a rambling old house. A quiet, tree-lined, residential neighborhood that smelled almost like Granny's fields of clover and wild strawberries. I learned later it was night-blooming jasmine, a far cry from the soap factory.

By the time we arrived, both Danny and I were grumpy and tired—the result of the sugar injection at Stuckey's and the uncertainty of our situation.

I dragged the shopping bag with my clothes and my special pink pillow up the stairs to the landing, stopping to look down at a family at the dinner table in the big house below. They were clinking glasses, the way I'd seen in movies, and eating from dinner plates with gold bands around the outside.

"They must be really rich," I said to no one in particular.

My dad said, "Hurry up!" and I turned and climbed the rest of the steps. We dumped the bags in the kitchen and hustled back down the stairs to take more from the trunk.

"Where do we sleep, Daddy?" my brother called out from the open window.

I was wondering the same thing. There were four rooms, all about the same size, and only one double bed.

"You'll be in there with me," he said, "and Janet can have the couch in the living room."

It wasn't a real couch, just a daybed, draped with a plaid cover and stacked with pillows to look like a couch.

Later, in the darkness of night, I thought about our life here.

Would city people be friendly, like those at Stuckey's? What would the new school be like? Would I have another best friend, like Phyllis? Would the other girls like me? Would I have the right clothes? What was I supposed to do, without Mom or Granny around?

As I stretched out on the thin mattress, there was something old and musty-smelling about the pillows, like they'd been in a flood and dried out.

"I'm glad I have my own pillow," I thought to myself and threw the others to the floor.

It was too hot to sleep. I tossed. I turned. I got out of the well-used bed, sat on the open window sill for awhile, and looked down the driveway to the houses across the way. They were all big, two or three stories, separated by driveways. Soft lights filtered through shutters and sheer curtains. A dog barked nearby and was scolded by someone with a deep voice.

Laughter from the house below caught my attention, and I watched an older woman clearing the table, walking back and forth, in and out of my sight line. Then, the lights went out, and I sat for awhile, in the stillness, hearing my father's soft snore. I sat, half-asleep, lost in the scent of night jasmine and orange blossom, listening to the sound of wind in the palm trees. A different sound from the wind that played with the silver maples near Granny's porch.

I went back to the daybed, thinking that any town that smelled this good couldn't be all bad. I would make it work.

I fell asleep, saying over and over to myself, "I'll make it work. I'll make it work."

The next morning, I woke up drenched in sweat, almost gagging from the heat and humidity. I could hear a faint hum and realized my dad had a fan going somewhere. He was at the small dining room table, drinking coffee and reading the papers.

"What time is it?" I asked and headed for the bathroom.

"It's early. You don't have to go to school today; we'll go down later and get you and Danny enrolled."

Daddy was putting away the milk when I got back to the kitchen. He handed me a Little Debbie oatmeal cake and nodded to the glass of milk he'd put out for me on the dining table, next to the rotating fan.

"Are you going to work?"

"Not today. Tomorrow."

He turned the papers to the comics section and began to read *Dagwood and Blondie*, his lips moving slightly as he read to himself.

I interrupted.

"What do we tell people?" I asked, as I dipped a piece of cake into the milk.

"What do you mean?"

"What do we tell people at school when they ask about Mom?"

The fan had caught some of his papers and blown them onto the floor. He quietly picked them up, folded the paper in half, and sat back down across from me. He was already dressed in his khaki pants and short sleeved blue shirt. Cigarettes in the left pocket. He read for a couple of minutes, sighed heavily and looked at me. His eyes, black-rimmed from all the years in the coal mines, looked frightened.

"I don't know. What do you want to tell them?"

"I don't know."

I could hear Danny stretching and whimpering in the next room.

"We could tell them she's taking care of her mother, up in Virginia," he said softly.

I shot him a look, like, "Are you telling me to lie?" and he shrugged.

Nobody I'd ever known up to 1953 had parents who didn't live together. Oh, maybe one or the other was dead or in the hospital or something, but no one I knew was in this situation.

I couldn't find the words to describe it.

"Is she coming back?" I licked the icing from the middle of the cake.

"I don't know. She said she might."

He drained the coffee from his cup and got up to put the cup in the sink. He leaned against the sink, looking into the living room, where all the covers and pillows were on the floor. He didn't say anything; just stood and stared.

Finally, just to put a lid on my rising nervousness, just to fill the hurting space, I agreed.

"We'll tell them she has a sick mother and has to be with her. That way, if she comes back, it won't be so weird."

My dad nodded his head, picked up his paper, and left the room.

New Friends

1954, Tampa, Florida

My new girlfriend was always in a hurry. "We're going to miss the bus. Come on, slowpoke! Lord, I don't know how I hooked up with the slowest person in the neighborhood!"

Always rushing ahead, while the steps I took were measured.

"You're not in the country anymore; stop your lollygagging. Let's go already!"

I wouldn't have described myself as slow, but, then, Myra had grown up in the city and always seemed to be thrashing about, ordering people around in her wake. She had a way of getting right up in peoples' faces and asking the most personal questions, like, "How come you do your eyes that way? Have you ever thought about wearing blue eye shadow instead of green? It'd make your eyes look bigger; you really should try it!"

If pressed, I would have described myself as shy, uncertain. I was walking on new terrain, far removed from the smell of tobacco and musty autumn mountains, the slate-covered, smoky coal fields of West Virginia.

Tampa was paved all over; it had street lights, with people out walking night and day; supermarkets that were open for twenty four hours. Yet, it was the sweetest-smelling place I'd ever lived. Not even Granny's apple orchards coated with purple, spring clover could compete.

It was the whisper of jasmine and orange blossoms, occasionally punctuated by gardenias. That scent would shift my entire focus to whatever direction it came from. Sometimes at night, I roamed the wide streets alone, under protection of the tulip trees and magnolias, just to find a fragrant trail, follow it, stand quietly, and lose myself, happy and smiling and glad to be there.

Myra didn't know about these evening walks. She was always too busy anyway. A year and a half older but only one grade ahead of me, we walked to school together most mornings, and she'd disclose secret tales about other girls in her seventh grade class. She'd talk all the way to school but hardly speak to me when we passed in the hallway between classes. After all, she was a seventh-grader.

I'd never known anyone like her. She told me she was Jewish, which I understood to be something like Hungarian or Italian but more so. She was the first girl I knew who had pierced ears, and I thought the piercing identified her as Jewish.

I'd watch for Myra at the end of the day, scurry over, and fall in step, just to have company and be seen with someone who seemed so popular at school. I barely knew my way around the school building, let alone the neighborhood, whereas Myra seemed to know all the business going on in one house or another.

"That's where John Davis lives; he's the class president. Joanne Adderly used to live there but she got pregnant and had to move away. You should have known her; she was W-I-L-D," she emphasized, snapping her gum, and patting her heavily-sprayed, blond bob.

"Sue Reynolds lives over there. Now, her family has MONEY, honey!"

Clearly we didn't. I was still wearing oxfords and the wrap-around brown skirt I'd sewn when I was at Granny's. I couldn't help notice that girls at school wore sling backs and nylons with their matching outfits.

After a couple of months, Dad got word that Mom was going to join us in Tampa. I didn't know why. I know she told my dad she wasn't living in any garage apartment, that he'd better find a better place. So, he did.

We moved from the garage apartment in the back, to the duplex of the big house in front. Dad explained that we could stay in the same schools that way. The living room of the new apartment had a couch that became two single beds at night, and that's where Danny and I were to sleep.

I wasn't excited about her coming; I'd learned to get along without her and dreaded her clinging, emotional behavior. We went on about our daily lives, not knowing when she might show up.

The entrance to our new apartment was to the left of the main door of the house, where Myra lived with an aunt and uncle and two young cousins. Myra's bright pink bedroom on the first floor overlooked the driveway, which was convenient when she wanted to sneak out to meet boys at the end of the block, she teased. Over her canopied bed were two, small, autographed photos of the Everly Brothers. On one of my rare visits to her room, she told me she'd actually been to an Everly Brothers concert up in Ybor City last year.

"It was so exciting! My girlfriends and I ate in one of those fancy Cuban restaurants and my mom let us all have a sip of her wine. My dad was teasing all the girls about how he could sing better than the Everly Brothers. It was our best family time!"

It's the only time I remember her talking about her parents. I found out later from the kids at the Community Center that her parents had drowned. The kids all felt sorry for her.

Myra seldom wanted to play or hang out once we were home from school. She had to help her aunt with the boys and she had a part-time job at the Community Center on Handler Avenue. She hardly ever asked me anything about myself or where my mom was, and she never wanted to come into my side of the house when I asked.

She did ask me to go to the pool with her once. I was invited because her best friend was sick and Myra didn't want to ride the bus alone. At least that's what she told me.

"Come on, those boys are heading to the pool and we'll never catch up with them if you don't get a move on."

"I'm trying. I can't run because the poison ivy hurts when my legs rub together!"

"Oh, god, what am I doing with you?"

I suffered her attitude in silence, too scared to risk losing the only friend I had at the time.

Once at the pool, Myra selected the perfect spot, spread her towel, and stepped out of her shorts and tee shirt to reveal a new, two-piece suit.

"Isn't it wonderful?" she gushed, adjusting her full-grown breasts into the small top.

I had to admit it was. The boys nearby agreed with nods and smiles and *V for Victory* signs.

My own suit was a red, one-piece, strapless faille that had belonged to my mother. I liked it. Or at least I did until I saw Myra's. I had nothing to fill out the top, but it did stay up without straps. I liked that.

In short order, the boys edged closer and Myra was cracking gum and laughing and refreshing her red lipstick, calling out to the boys she knew. She didn't bother introducing me and no one came over to my side of the blanket. One of the boys offered to put sun lotion on her back and she winked at me and turned to the side.

I studied the poison ivy behind my knees and was glad to see it was clearing up. I applied a little calamine lotion over the area and rolled onto my stomach, thinking the sun would be good for the small blisters.

I must have dozed off for awhile, for when I opened my eyes, I was coated in sweat and Myra was gone. I could hear her laugh and guessed she was in the pool with the boys.

Wandering toward a shady spot on the edge of the pool, I was nearly run over by two guys following the beach ball they were trying to keep in the air.

"Sorry," said the tall, thin one.

"Hey, watch you don't run the pretty lady down," said the browner, muscular one.

I stepped around the ball, mumbling something like "It's okay," and they continued their game. I kept them in my sights as I eased down to the edge of the pool where I could look around for Myra and see them out of the corner of my eye at the same time.

The chlorine water felt good against the itchy patches behind my knees.

The beach ball made a small splash as it hit the water, and the boys' impromptu jumps after it made me squeal and cower from them. The tall, thin boy got the ball and looked around, but his friend was waist-high in the pool, walking toward me.

"I'm sorry," he said, wiping his face with his arm, "We didn't mean to mess with you but it looks like we're doing a good job of it."

I smiled, wondering if he was talking to me or someone behind me.

He jumped up on the ledge, and I could feel the coolness of his wet skin a few inches away as he settled close by. His friend took his time walking over, smiling and balancing the ball on one finger.

"My name's Raphael, but you can call me Ralph," said the one beside me. "What's yours?"

I told him my name.

"Pretty name, pretty lady," he nodded to his friend. "This here's my friend, Jerry. Geraldo, really, but he goes by Jerry."

"Hello."

"Where you from? Where you go to school?" Ralph asked.

"We just moved here," I said. "I go to Woodrow Wilson."

"Oh, yea, we know that school. We go to St. Catherine's, north side of town. Remember, Jerry, we played for that dance over at Wilson a few months ago?"

Jerry nodded.

"Maybe you were there," Ralph teased. "We play in a Cuban band; I play trumpet and my friend here is our bass player."

"No, I wasn't there. I only moved here in April."

"Oh, well, you'll have to come hear us play sometime. You like *Cherry Pink & Apple Blossom White*? That's the kind of music we play. We have lots of fun. We dance. My friend and I can come pick you up sometime. Okay? I don't mean no disrespect, either. It's just a party."

I know there were other words exchanged. They're just lost in the weight of memory about those years.

I told Ralph I was fourteen, adding only a year to the birthday I'd had just a few weeks earlier.

"It's because of the change in schools," I explained, that I was only "going into the seventh grade."

He was sixteen and was already in high school. He liked me; I could tell.

"My friend and I have to go pick up my father," Ralph eventually said. "Tell me where you live and I'll come see you sometime after school. I drive my own scooter."

I gave him the address.

"Okay, *te veo*, Juanita."

"A real pleasure," Jerry smiled, as he followed his friend.

I sat there, watching them go, reliving the moments and listening to Nat King Cole from someone's portable radio:

Blue velvet. Bluer than velvet were her eyes. Warmer than May her tender sighs . . .

My heart was racing.

"Aaaagh!" Myra yelled as she splashed at me. "Wake up, silly! Who was that you were talking to?"

"Nobody," I shrugged. "Just a boy."

"C-U-T-E if you ask me! Where's he from? He looks Cuban."

I turned away from her.

"I know how to speak Spanish," I lied. "We were just talking."

I stood up and stretched in the sun, feeling an edge I'd not had before.

"It's getting late," I said. "I think we should go soon," and rushed to retrieve the towel that would warm the shivers I suddenly felt.

Looking for Love

1954-1955, Tampa, Florida

My neighborhood friends were likely the first generation of latchkey kids, long before the phrase had been popularized by sociologists and the media. Some of us had one parent around; others had both parents working—very different from my experience in rural Virginia or in the mountains. There, people had extended families with someone always watching out for the kids, helping out with the chores. And there was little time to do nothing.

Since there wasn't much family around, we kids relied on each other. We roamed the streets in the evenings, our parents glad for a little peace and quiet; us, happy to be out of the house, glad for the freedom.

By this time, I had developed something of a shadow self.

One part of me I showed in public or around my parents. Another, inside my head or with occasional friends. Thought I

119

didn't know it then, I was learning to compartmentalize my life as self-protection.

I had learned to follow the rules in public, but, in my private life, I was often one step over that line, pushing the limits, experimenting.

With the neighborhood kids, I'd do things like sneak up to someone's window at night and make ghost noises or shadow someone walking down a dark street, just to scare them. My favorite thing was jumping from elevators in the new, high rise apartment buildings. I'd learned to stop the elevator between floors, force open the door and jump onto the hallway floor below. I'd dare the gang to join me, and we'd go down a floor each time until we reached the vestibule or until one of the tenants caught on and yelled at us or called the superintendent. No one ever fell through the shaft, though it was a good possibility. I loved the excitement and the adrenaline rush.

I also liked having a gang of friends. We could disagree, even argue, but we all found our way back to each other during the year or two I lived in Tampa. Latchkey kids on the prowl.

One friend in our group took our wild ways too far and got himself arrested. Five or six of us were hanging out, wanting to go somewhere but too young to drive. One of the boys had just turned sixteen, and he volunteered to get his parents' car. We watched as he strutted down the block and went inside his house. We waited. And waited. And waited.

Suddenly a police car, with lights flashing, pulled up in front of his house. We stayed where we were, anxious to know what had happened, but unwilling to get any closer. The police brought him out in handcuffs, put him in the patrol car, and drove off. We found out later that our friend, Grant, had pulled a shotgun on his parents when they refused to give him the keys. I never saw him for the rest of the time I lived there.

Back in Virginia, and even West Virginia, the worst trouble my friends and I ever got into—outside of home—was at Halloween. We'd throw sandbags on people's porches, even maybe fill the paper bag with dog poop and throw it at their houses. Turn over garbage cans, soap windows and throw porch rugs onto the roof. Once we even pushed over somebody's outhouse!

But here in the big city, there were more dangerous opportunities for trouble.

One evening, when I was fourteen, a girlfriend agreed to help me stalk the sixteen year-old I had a crush on. Around ten o'clock one Friday night, we hid out in the dark alley where Ward parked his car. We were sure we'd find him with a girl. We'd been there only five minutes or so when we were flooded with car lights from both sides. A male voice called out, asking what we were doing. In seconds we were surrounded by four men, detectives they said, asking for our names and why we were there.

Somehow, I blurted out the story.

"I think my boyfriend is seeing somebody else, and I wanted to know for sure."

My friend, Carolyn, and I were starting to cry about now, surprised and terrified we'd been caught and certain we'd be reported, if not jailed. The men had scoped out the alley, anticipating a drug deal, they said. We were caught in the middle. They told us to get on home and not do this again. No worry there!

It was while we were in Tampa that I discovered people thought I was pretty. I'd never thought much about it, never focused on it by wearing lipstick or seductive clothes. My breasts were nothing to look at, and I was tall and lanky. Someone at the after-school Community Center nominated me to be a princess in the annual Gasparilla Celebration, and I was selected to represent the center.

With my mom still living across the state, I turned to one of the center staff for advice. Mrs. Martin found a neighbor who gave me one of her formal dresses to wear; another loaned me her shoes. A girlfriend's mother did my hair. I was proud to ride on the Gasparilla Queen's float in the downtown Tampa parade and to be escorted to the evening dance by another friend's brother. I liked being thought of as pretty; it created opportunities that I never would have thought about.

The handsome Cuban boy I'd met at the pool started coming by after school and, one day, asked if I'd go steady with him.

"I'll have to ask my dad," I told him, not even thinking about what I wanted. I just knew I liked the way Rafael smelled and the sounds he made when he spoke Spanish. I liked the latte color of his skin.

Later that evening, my dad sat in his comfortable chair, humming a Frank Sinatra song and reading the paper. He was in a good mood because my mother had written she'd be *home* within a few weeks. I sat on the foot stool next to him, told him Raphael had asked me to go steady, and could I?

He put his paper on his lap and looked at me for what seemed like minutes, but was, most likely, a few seconds.

"Well, I don't know," he said, thoughtfully. "What does it mean to go steady?"

He didn't ask about Raphael's being Cuban; he didn't ask where he was from or what his parents did. He wanted to know, from me, what it meant. He wanted me to define the relationship.

I couldn't ever remember being asked what I wanted, and it nearly took my breath away.

"It means he can come over after school, and we can go to the movies together," I said quickly, making it up to suit myself.

I could see he was thinking it over, and I sat on my hands, biting my lip.

"I guess it's okay, but you'll have to take your brother with you when you go to the movies."

I threw my arms around him, scrunching the paper.

"Thank you, Daddy; thank you. I will!"

Over the years, I've remembered this scene with deep fondness for my father. What a wise man he was in that moment.

Raphael and I went steady for exactly one week and three days, long enough for me to learn to say: *"Oye, te amo mucho. Darme un besita ahorita!"* Hey, I love you a lot. Give me a little kiss right now!

During that week and three days, he had come over after school four times; taken me to a dance party, where he and Jerry played in the Cuban band; and then taken my brother and me to a movie. In the movie he put his arm around me, and Danny, who was sitting behind us, whispered loudly, "I'm going to tell Dad."

Raphael laughed and left his arm where it was.

Soon enough, Raphael met another girl. She was a year older than I and had bigger boobs, and it didn't bother me much. Anyway, I could see that his friend, Jerry, liked me and he was much taller than Ralph. My dad asked which one I liked better and I said, "I like both of them; mostly I just want to keep going to the dance parties!"

Raphael and Jerry and I stayed friendly, and I was often part of a group invited to the Cuban dance parties on weekends, initiating a love of Spanish culture and music and language that lingers to this day.

I guess sometimes the ground can shift between your feet.
Sometimes your footing slips. You stumble. And sometimes you
grab what's close to you and hold on as tight as you can.

The Wonder Years

A New Understanding

1955-1956, Tampa
1957, West Virginia
1958, West Palm Beach
1959, West Virginia

Making close friends had never come easily for me. It took time; and we were seldom in one place long enough to explore relationships and weigh them.

I was tough on the outside but, inside, I was actually quite shy, never sure of myself with new people. Going to a new school each year—and sometimes doubling back to one I'd been to a few years earlier—I had to work at making friends in order to survive the loneliness, that feeling of being out of place, not belonging. The kids at school had known each other for years and there were hundreds of stories among them. I didn't know their stories and they didn't know mine, not that I was eager to tell mine. I had become a good survivor by the time I was fourteen, good at denial and hiding and

125

being secretive when necessary, but it was difficult to go beyond that. Except in my head. In my imagination, I travelled the world, had romances, good friends, and interesting conversations.

At times I felt like two people, two personalities: competent and polite in some situations; insecure, watchful, frigid with fear in others. I wondered at times if I was crazy, like my mother. I never talked about this. I didn't know how to. I was unable to fathom, let alone share, such ideas. Mother was on edge most of the time, and I was quite aware that she could leave, upend the family at any moment.

Then, we'd have to start over again.

At a new school in Florida, I noticed this one boy—class president, honor student, Mr. Popular—and saw that he spoke to nearly everyone he passed in the hall, calling them by name. I decided to pattern myself after him, make friends that way.

"I can do that," I thought, and began to practice with kids in my homeroom.

"Hey Mary, how're you doing? Hi Bob, how was gym today?"

People responded, even liked it that I spoke first.

Not realizing it, I had learned an important skill: drawing others to me by showing interest in them.

This initiative came out of intention, however, not confidence. The behavior was well-intended and contributed to a persona that seemed to work for me. It was me, but not me. I could avoid talking about anything personal, like feelings, but I could fit into new situations and make small talk.

It helped ease some of that aching loneliness, that feeling of not being connected to anyone.

Soon enough I returned to Logan High School in the tenth grade, and, using my new skill, discovered people liked me and looked up to me. I had gone to middle school with many of these students, and they expected me to be stuck up, having lived in the big city and all. But they discovered I wasn't; I appeared interested in them. They seemed to need the attention and acceptance as much as I did.

1957 began as a very good sophomore year.

However, it wasn't long before my mother uprooted the family again, leaving my father and brother behind in West Virginia, taking me with her to West Palm Beach. Again, all new people, this time at Palm Beach High School in a much bigger city than even Tampa.

Mom worked the dinner shift at a fancy restaurant, and I often was by myself and lonely beyond words. It may have been my first experience with depression. My new, learned skill of small talk lay dormant under the heavy feeling of being lost, unconnected. I couldn't invite classmates over for fear I'd have to explain where the rest of my family was. I felt ashamed, somehow.

I was never lonelier than in this period of my life, watching television from the time I got home from school until I went to bed, sometimes crying myself to sleep, praying for the hurt and loneliness to stop.

I called my brother and Granny Bill as often as Mom would let me. She didn't like me calling them when she wasn't around.

"I wanted to talk to them, too," she'd whine

I think she was worried about what I'd tell them in her absence. All I'd do was cry and beg them to let me come home.

They never did.

I went to church a lot. There were youth groups and choir practices, and, even here, I felt like such a loner. I did look forward to going to Catholic Mass occasionally with Mom's boyfriend, Fred, whenever he was around. Mom never wanted to go to church. She said she'd go the day she stopped drinking and, "It ain't gonna be today!"

The rituals of the Catholic Church, the smell of incense and candles, always fascinated me and calmed me down. So different from the fire-and-brimstone Pentacostal Churches I'd gone to up north.

Fred and I would stop for donuts on the way home, and he'd ask me about school and the books I was reading, what I enjoyed most. He seemed interested. I liked Fred above all Mom's boyfriends.

In the middle of the eleventh grade social studies class, the teacher asked if anyone would be interested in attending a monthly luncheon at the Breakers Hotel in Palm Beach, where a small group of educated men and women would meet to discuss art, history, and issues of the day. They were looking to sponsor a student. My hand was up before she finished her sentence, and, as a result, I was excused from classes once a month and picked up by an adult who drove me to the Palm Beach Breakers Hotel for lunch and back again.

I don't remember the names of any of the people in that group of twenty or so, but, in retrospect, some might be familiar today. Some spoke French; others, Spanish. I learned about their art collections. I saw pictures of their homes in Paris and Madrid and California. They talked of sailing on the Queen Mary or lounging in sleeping rooms on fast-moving trains. They discussed books they'd read and famous people they'd met, what they'd worn to this ball or that. They spoke of civil rights and politics and education and of doing the right thing. Some, I learned, had been doctors and businessmen in Cuba before emigrating to Florida, before *the revolutionary activities* gained strength. I wanted to know more about this revolution that was developing in their nearby country, but no one at lunch seemed to want to talk about it

It was at The Breakers where I discovered that the extra fork on the table was for salad; the spoon laid parallel to the table's edge, above my plate, was for dessert; and a cloth napkin belonged on my lap, not tucked into my shirt. I learned to eat cauliflower with a sweet, melted cheese sauce and *haricot verts*, neither of which I'd heard of or tasted before. A whole new world was opening to me, and I loved every minute of it.

These adults wanted to know what I thought, what my plans were; they encouraged me to question things, and they answered my questions. If I didn't have an opinion, they suggested books to get from the library or someone would bring me a book the following month. There was no subtlety, no deviousness between us.

Their attention and affection, however light, felt genuine.

My curiosity, my dreaming self came to life. I wasn't lonely there. I wanted to know everything. Were there really café tables in the streets of Paris? Could you actually sleep on a fast-moving train? What was so special about this opera or that dance performance? Why did this artist just throw paint on a canvas? I relived these experiences every night after our meetings, waiting for my mother to come home from the restaurant. If Fred were with her, he always wanted to hear what had happened at The Breakers and seemed pleased for me.

I tried once to tell Mom about the lunch group, when Fred wasn't around, but she was too tired to listen or didn't care. She'd throw out, "Don't go getting above your raising, Miss Priss," which cut to the bone.

Why was it wrong to want to learn something new, something beautiful, I wondered? Why couldn't she talk to me about what I cared about? Rather than risk her criticism, I kept my excitement to myself and dreamed of the next meeting.

Privately, I wrote in my diary, that "getting above my raising" was exactly what I wanted!

These lunches brought to life a sense of beauty and style I had only dreamed of or read about in magazines. It was the beginning of an emerging self, where intelligence and feelings came together, where life made sense to me. I barely recognized this new person, but I liked her.

Once again, however, life was upended when my mother decided we were going back to West Virginia. Surprisingly, I was upset about returning home. I was beginning to find my place here. She didn't want to hear it.

"All you ever say is how much you miss everybody. Why are you upset now?" she said, walking into the next room, never waiting for my response.

Fred was the one who seemed to understand how torn I was, between missing my family and loving this new world I'd found.

After church one Sunday, stopping for donuts at our favorite diner, Fred told me how lucky I was to have had this experience at The Breakers; something that made me feel good about myself and life and what life can be. I'll never forget his words.

"Once you've tasted that," he said, "you'll find it again. It's in you. You raised your hand in class and look what you found! You'll always know what a cauliflower with sweet cheese tastes like."

We laughed together, and he offered me his handkerchief for the tear stains on my face.

"If you want art and music and books in your life, or anything else, for that matter, you can have it. You can create it. Remember that."

I wanted so much to believe him, I began to cry again. I knew I'd miss this, having someone who would talk to me like this. I knew I'd miss Fred.

That morning, he turned my face to look me in the eye, and said, "Your mother never has and probably never will find exactly what she wants."

He said this kindly, not with a mean spirit.

"She keeps searching and wishing, and she thinks she's found it for awhile, but it evaporates, then she's disappointed again. She thinks it's outside her somewhere, like a dream. She doesn't know what you know: you really can *create* your own life if you want it badly enough. And I think you do."

I couldn't believe he was saying this to me. No one had ever been so honest, so clear about my mother and me.

He continued, almost whispering, saying things about my mother being like a little girl, always dreaming that something, or someone, will come along and make her happy.

"She's so scared inside, she can't figure out what she wants. That doesn't make her a bad person; it's just hard for her to think about anyone but herself. If anyone is happy or successful around her, she's jealous, because she doesn't know how to get it. You do, that's the difference."

He stopped for a moment, knowing this was a lot for me to take in, then said, "She thinks this time, things will be okay with your dad. I hope they are, for her sake and for yours."

I leaned into his chest and let the tears fall.

It was obvious that Mother wasn't happy with my dad, but he was familiar to her; he was family. He was her safety net. She felt secure with him until she didn't or until the security bored her; and then, she'd be off again, searching for that feeling of being alive.

Freedom's just another word for nothing left to lose.

Janis Joplin

Breaking Free

1958-1962, Logan and Huntington, West Virginia

Back at Logan High School for my senior year in 1958, the buzz started as soon as classes began.

"Janet's back. Have you seen Janet? She's back from Florida."

Even though I missed Fred and the conversations at The Breakers, I was happy to be home, happy to be around people I'd known over time.

That senior year was my best ever, for it had a sense of normalcy about it. Granny Bill had paid good money to have a new ranch house built for my parents, across the creek from the Pioneer, in the flat bottom, on Hatfield land. It was a beautiful house with a large picture window, very modern, unlike any of the other houses on Route 119. Granny hoped this new home might cement my parents' relationship. It didn't, but it kept them together for nearly two years.

It was certainly better than living in coal camp houses or garage apartments, and it was across the creek from Granny's.

Perhaps because of all I'd experienced outside of West Virginia, my confidence began to grow once we were back.

I connected with old friends, girls I had known, off and on, since grade school. They brought me up to date with the hundreds of stories that had transpired while I was away. *Susanne had gotten pregnant and dropped out of school. Wanda had had a nervous breakdown. So-and-so ran off with some trucker.*

I was connecting with them again.

I was seventeen and dependable enough to drive my dad's car, which allowed me to escape the tension in the house and participate in after-school activities. I joined every club I was eligible for, ignoring my mother's frequent comments about "Charity begins at home!" I sang in the high school chorus, encouraged by the avid enthusiasm of our choral director. There were times, however, she'd look at me, put her finger to her lips, and smile as the others carried the song and I lip-synched a difficult passage. We understood each other.

Because I was a good student, I was encouraged to take the college prep track. I was easily persuaded to take Latin, because I loved getting lost in the Roman and Greek myths and stories we read. I couldn't wait to read more about Ulysses; he had all these wonderful, exciting journeys that I loved learning about.

I had the self-assurance to try out for and win the lead in the senior play, playing a bride and wearing someone's trailing white gown. It was a big hit.

My classmates voted me Homecoming Queen, and I rode in back of a convertible with Mayor Litz McGuire in the downtown parade and onto the football field. I was Homecoming Queen without a date for the dance. It was awkward. But my girlfriends encouraged me to ask the best dancer in school, whom I barely knew, and I did. He agreed for whatever reason, and we spent a tense evening, hardly saying a word to each other; just dancing. Very awkward. Shouldn't the Queen have a boyfriend?

One success led to another. Where did this surge of optimism and intention come from? Had the low points and high ones in my past sculpted this person? Had I taken Fred's words to heart and begun to create a life I wanted? I gobbled up every opportunity, starved for connection.

It was as if my personality changed almost overnight, chameleon-like. I was determined to be the best. I enrolled in speech class, my heart set on winning the statewide competition against every high school dramatist in West Virginia. The speech teacher seemed to think I was special. He took an interest and helped me practice. My material for the statewide meet was a story about a mother who scrubbed floors at school, just to have the money for her daughter to attend. The daughter was disdainful and unappreciative. The mother died. It was soppy and sentimental.

The speech teacher, another student, and I drove to Morgantown for the competition, spending the night in dorms. There were contestants from all over the state. I came in second, which disappointed me a little but which made my teacher very proud. The winner told a highly dramatic story that ended with a song: *H A Double R I, G A N spells Harrigan*! She had the brash to pull it off, and I had to agree with the judges.

Another reason I took speech classes was because I'd discovered something about words. Words could change reality; words could be used to create a different perspective; they could be used to persuade people to do things: a handy strategy when moving in and out of different worlds.

The right word brought with it a feeling that drugs would never come close to creating. The word *chic,* for example. Such a little word that could express so much: elegance, style, New York, Paris! Words could transport me to other worlds. I loved the word *jasmine.* I liked to stretch out the z sound when I said it. Jazzzmine. With that word, I could see and inhale and feel the silkiness of the small white flower and knew exactly where I'd been when I discovered it.

A simple word like *yes* carried a world of meanings: one intonation could mean *let's get it done.* Another might suggest *I'll get to it someday.* And yet another, *I'm agreeing but don't mean it.* I was beginning to understand nuance. I was moving away from the rigidity of right or wrong rules and moving toward subtlety and beauty. It was like magic for me.

In my mother's house, there was no subtlety. Either I agreed with her and did what she said or there was trouble. No discussion. Children were to be seen and not heard.

I liked my teachers at school; they noticed and encouraged me, even suggesting I research colleges and apply for scholarships. No one in our family had gone to college. I was in love with the idea. The recognition that came from others when I accomplished something was a heady, validating feeling.

The feeling *inside*, however, meant more than others' acclamations ever could. I knew my eyes were brighter and my spine straighter when I got good grades or positive comments on a paper or presentation. I could see the value of setting goals and working to accomplish them. I was developing a voice, a perspective that was mine.

Fred was right. I could create my own life. I didn't have to be stuck in the world of my parents' drama.

That year in high school was special, too, because, shortly after Homecoming, I had a boyfriend, my first real boyfriend.

Jack was one of the nicest and most popular guys in school: good-looking, smart enough to be valedictorian, well-liked, focused, and funny, and he pursued me. He wanted *me*. He grew up with his mother and step-father in an apartment in downtown Logan and seemed to know everyone in town. He would drive the fifteen miles up Route 119 to pick me up at my house, drive us back to Logan for a movie or dance or church event, drive me home in the darkness, then back again.

I cared for Jack in an easy way I'd never felt for anyone else other than my brother and grandmother. I was learning about caring for someone outside the family. We talked about the future, about what we were reading, what we wanted to do with our lives. He had a part-time job at the radio station in town, which ignited his desire to be in broadcasting. He has succeeded quite well at it, but that's another story.

Jack enjoyed sitting and *shooting the bull* with my father, who sometimes slipped him a small glass of Manischewitz wine, making Dad very cool in Jack's eyes. It bothered me that he seemed to like my family more than I did, but there were secrets he didn't know about.

When he'd ask why I was so angry with my parents, I'd change the subject with a casual "Too much to ever tell!" How could I explain my mother's suffocating emotionality, her dramatic ups and downs; the reasons behind her affairs and running off?

I couldn't.

How could I explain to Jack why my father drank so much and, when he did, why he'd accuse me of being, "Just like your mother, too damned independent."

How could I explain my feelings when my drunken father would call me by my mother's name? I felt as if I didn't exist, I didn't matter to him anymore. I couldn't explain what had happened to the loving father of my younger days, the one who tried to keep the family together, the one who taught me to write and dance and love music; who let me go steady with a Cuban boy.

"Too much to ever tell!"

My mother, in her odd way, was proud of my accomplishments. She wanted me to be the perfect daughter, the one who was bright, pretty, well-mannered; the one who could present a sane, positive reflection of our life to the world. The daughter who hid the ugly truths behind a sweet smile or a "Thank you, ma'am."

It was an unspoken contract we had; I presented an accomplished, normal, pretty girl to the world, and kept my feelings to myself. Who I was on the outside seldom reflected what was going on inside.

My mother loved to show me off, as if I were her doll, her accomplishment.

"Come in here and show Mrs. Smith how I did your hair this morning."

I hated it. I had begun to hate her.

Even as I struggled to escape the web she'd created for us for too many years, I was still her confidant, her holder of secrets. To deny her openly was to face her wrath.

So, I became her enabler.

"Of course, I love you. You're my mother."

Her sounding board.

"I think he'd like you better in the low-cut dress."

Her excuse.

"Dad, she was late because of me."

I was beginning to see the larger picture, how I'd been drawn in, but I didn't have the words or ability to break through yet. And I was scared.

I kept all this to myself. Yet I wondered, as I read the tragedies of Shakespeare and the Greeks, whether I, too, wasn't trapped in some kind of tragic drama. The story of Orestes—the plotting and revenge of his father's death by killing his adulterous mother—left me terrified that I had, indeed, inherited a catastrophic life. Knowing that my mother's blood flowed through my veins was almost too much to consider.

Way too much to tell.

When Jack and I weren't involved in after-school activities or going to church together, we hung out in the semi-finished basement of our new ranch house, talking and grinding to the teen tragedies of 1958 and '59: The Flamingos singing *I Only Have Eyes for You;* Sam Cooke with *You Send me, Teen Angel, Tell Laura I Love Her;* The Drifters, The Penguins and more. Black music had emerged into white culture, Elvis was king, and life was full of romantic ideas at seventeen.

Jack and I were easy together. He wrote me love notes; we grabbed short kisses in the hallway between classes, but I was strictly a first-base girl. I suspected that some of my girlfriends were going further, much further, but I remained something of a prude, a good girl. Not that we didn't slide into second base from time to time. Doing so always raised too many feelings, too much guilt for me, so I'd insist we backtrack to first.

139

Given what I'd seen in my life, it was all or nothing when it came to sex. I'd seen my mother's depression, her antipathy to my father's advances, their fights in the middle of the night, her calling him an animal. I'd also seen her exhilaration and high spirits when there was someone new in her life.

In my mind, sex was larger than life, overwhelming and threatening. Sex brought with it the lies and betrayal and damage I'd seen in my family—a tsunami of wreckage and destruction, wounding and devastating everyone in its wake. I was too scared to open the floodgate.

At seventeen, I was content to leave that upheaval locked away.

Having a boyfriend, kissing and rubbing against one another, was fun, and Jack was patient and persistent at the same time. Once, when I was wearing a scooped neck sweater, Jack and I made out for what seemed like hours on my living room couch, my parents asleep not thirty feet away, him kissing my neck over and over, moving slowly toward my breasts. Suddenly, a swell of emotion overtook me, and I experienced my first orgasm.

Amazing, I thought, but not earth-shattering. Still virginal, now I knew something of what everyone was so excited about. Was this the something that my mother kept searching for? Could this be it? It was a good feeling, shackled with some guilt, but nothing to break up a family for.

Soon enough, Jack gave me his class ring, we introduced our parents to each other, and everyone assumed we were engaged to be engaged. After graduating high school, he went off to a private college for boys in North Carolina, and we wrote and called and intended to be together in the future.

I don't remember much discussion about my going to college or about my being the first in the family to go. I drooled over a catalogue for Sullins College, a girls' junior college outside of Bristol, Virginia. The pictures brought back memories of The Breakers. One paragraph in the catalogue described Sullins as a private school that "attracted girls from wealthy families throughout the southeast."

Today I can only imagine how out of place I would have been there. My parents said no, we couldn't afford it.

Marshall University, sixty miles away from home, offered me a full scholarship.

My parents contributed $50 per month and I found a part-time job in a dress shop in Huntington. That sealed the deal, and I was off to major in Spanish and English, intending to get my teaching degree, a notable profession for girls in those days.

Again, I was in an entirely new environment, but this time, I was determined to make it mine. It was scary with all the new people, professors' expectations, and the freedom from family rules and drama. The drama, at least, had been familiar. I, at least, knew my place. But in this new world, my confidence was growing. Living away from home, having had a relatively normal year, I felt capable of making friends; capable to make everyday decisions about my life and what I wanted to do.

It was a heady experience. Even though I was only sixty miles from my parents, I could have been across the world. High school friends who attended Marshall typically went home on the weekends; they talked of being homesick and relishing time with their families, reminiscing about life before college.

Not me; I didn't want to think about the past. I wanted a future.

I always made up excuses for not going home on weekends. The person I was to ride with got sick. The car broke down. I had an exam. I had to work. My roommate and others on my floor helped hold my mother at bay. Everyone was in on it and some even needed the same.

"Oh, I'm sorry; she just left for the library. I'll tell her you called."

And Mother did call, two or three times every week to tell me what was going on with her, how much she missed me, how much she *needed* me to come home. I lied easily, without guilt. Her dependency on me had only intensified since I left, and it threatened to pull me back into the vortex of her craziness.

"I don't have anyone to talk to," she'd cry into the phone. "I need you to come home."

Granny Bill wrote that Mom was depressed all the time now, taking drugs and drinking more.

"She's downright pitiful," Granny said, "but don't you think about quitting school. You stay where you are . . . and call me if you need anything!"

For the most part, but not completely, I was able to put my mother and her problems out of my mind, treasuring my illusion of freedom. I worked and studied hard. My social life was minimal, since I was now *pinned* to Jack, but groups of us went to concerts and plays and I met people who'd travelled, who loved jazz and had friends across color lines.

Many of my professors had been strongly influenced by the European socialists, philosophers and writers—Sartre, Flaubert, Kierkegaard—and they challenged us to think critically about everything. I was caught up in the early civil rights movement in 1961-62, and we'd discuss and argue into the night about personhood and whether color made a difference. I struggled with the decision to march or not march, held back by that imprint to not make trouble, be a lady. Once, a group of us did try to desegregate the movie theatre in Huntington by taking one of our black friends with us. The woman in the ticket booth looked very nervous, quickly wrote a sign on bond paper, taped it to her window, and exited the booth. The sign said "No Negroes Allowed." We were so naïve and uninformed at the time, we all just turned around and headed back to campus, not knowing what to do. In retrospect, it was not my finest moment.

My family had always referred to themselves as Yellow Dog Democrats, a phrase used to describe Southerners who always voted the Democratic ticket. They were pro-union liberals in a fashion, and when asked, I joined the campus Democratic Club. In the spring of 1960, I was running for class senator at Marshall and had made business-card sized advertisements that said, "Vote for Janet Steele for Senator." All my friends pinned them to their matching sweater sets or button-down shirts.

One day the Young Democratic Club was notified that the national Democratic candidate for President was touring West Virginia and would be stopping by the campus. I stood in the front line and listened to John F. Kennedy speak from the hood of his car, telling hundreds of us his plans for West Virginia and the nation. He motioned to me and asked for a card.

Vote For

Janet Steele

For

SOPHOMORE

SENATOR

The future president held up my card and said—how can I ever forget it?—"Vote for Janet Steele for Senator and vote for this Senator for President!"

The crowd roared; we both won.

Those were exciting days for me, and I relished every moment. I continued to be involved in church, through the Campus Christian Center, but the ideas discussed there were far from my Pentecostal—even my hit-and-run Catholic—upbringing. In the campus church we talked as much about psychotherapy and literature as religion, reading D.H. Lawrence, Simone de Bouvier, Henry Thoreau, Emily Dickinson, and Rollo May's *Love and Will*.

One Friday, as friends and I were sauntering back to the freshman dorm after science class, there stood my mother outside the dormitory. I stopped dead in my tracks. Seeing the look on my face and my mother's fierce look, my friends scattered.

"You're coming home, by god! No more excuses," she shouted, moving toward me in a fury.

I tried to slip past her, but she followed close as we went into the dorm and up the stairs to my room.

"Who do you think you are?" she shouted. "Do you think you can disappear, forget about your family? You're coming home, young lady!"

Girls on the floor came to their doors to hear what the ruckus was about.

I threw dirty clothes into a shopping bag and headed back down the stairs. I said little on the way home. She was accusatory and making every effort to induce guilt.

"After all I've done for you, you'd think I could get some appreciation!"

What she'd done for me? She'd given me birth, shared her DNA, taught me to dress and act like a lady; I'm sure there was more. But at that moment, I felt nothing for her. I stared out at the road, at the familiar places along Route 10, going deeper into the dark mountains, as we neared home.

I saw her finally, as Granny had said, as sad and pitiful, but not so frightening anymore. It was as if I'd stepped outside my body. At some level, I could shut her out.

That weekend, I barely said a word. She talked on and on about herself, how lonely she was, how nobody paid attention to her. She cried that my father had failed her, that my brother was out running around and never home, and she was thinking of moving to Huntington, to be closer to me. When I heard that, I wanted to physically hurt her, do anything to drive her away from me. Instead, I walked into the hall closet, closed the door and cried into the winter coats that smelled of the past.

"I'm talking to you," she screeched outside the door. "Don't go acting crazy to get away from me."

I opened the door and stood there for a moment, suddenly calm, just staring at her.

"I *am* crazy," I said quietly. "You've made me crazy. Even the psychologist at school said . . ."

I didn't get all the words out before she grabbed my shoulders and shook me.

"What do you mean, psychologist? How could you talk to a stranger about this family? What's wrong with you anyway? Why aren't you telling me what's going on with you?"

As quickly as she was in my face, she shrugged and turned to walk away.

"There's nothing wrong with you except your damned uppity attitude. I won't have you talking to no psychologist ever again; do you hear me?"

I saw no way through this encounter and, in that moment, for the second time in my life, I imagined killing myself. Then, at least, it would all be over. And, it would hurt her.

I let her rant. I could see the drugs at work in her. She cared more about controlling my behavior than any truth I might bring to the situation. In the middle of it all, I called a friend and arranged a ride back to school that afternoon.

Mother had settled into sobbing and apologizing by the time my friend arrived.

"I'm so sorry, honey. I don't mean to hurt you. I just can't help myself. I'm just so lonely with you gone."

I ignored her. I threw my shopping bag into Joanne's car, slammed the door, and said, "Get me the hell out of here!"

I was drained of emotion. I felt like a tornado survivor, thrown into new territory with considerable injury and no idea what the future held. I knew we had crossed a line this weekend. I had nothing left for her, barely anything for myself. I was a blank page, a future full of question marks.

The school psychologist later asked where my father and Danny were during the tortuous night and day I was at home. I couldn't tell him; I was barely aware of their presence. They made themselves scarce, I guess. Nobody intervened, not even Granny Bill, who must have been told what was going on. I didn't go over to say hello or goodbye. I hadn't called Jack the way I usually did on Saturdays. Like that tornado victim, I had survived, but barely.

And there was way too much to tell.

Jack and I continued our relationship during holidays and summers through my freshman and sophomore years. He wrote beautiful letters about his life at school and persuaded me to come down for a fraternity dance weekend. I felt very grown up, sharing expenses with a friend and driving to Charlotte by ourselves. I recall a party at the Kappa Alpha house where we stepped over dozens of couples sprawled over the floor of a dark room. Everyone, except us, seemed to be drinking a lot. A huge snowstorm settled on Charlotte that weekend, and, with exams waiting for me, I took my first flight in a small fifteen-seater plane, both frightened and euphoric as I looked at the world through the clouds.

Somewhere during my junior year, I started to neglect Jack. Our future together seemed a century away, and I needed a more immediate escape plan. My mother had, in fact, moved to Huntington, gotten an apartment, and a waitressing job. She called regularly. She'd call after the restaurant closed, often in a drunken or drugged stupor. Now she was having visions and hearing voices in the walls. This was more serious than what her doctors had called *nerves*, but I didn't care anymore. Compassion and guilt had disappeared in my quest for a separate life. When she called, I'd let her talk on and on, then say I had to hang up and study. I couldn't engage any more.

She was drowning and I couldn't save her. I advised her to go see another doctor. I wanted out.

About the same time, I met a classmate in drama class who was two years older and had all the charisma of a charlatan, a rainmaker. Fool that I was, I fell head-over-heels for Royce*. Some would say I fell in love, but it wasn't love. It wasn't anything like I felt for Jack. It was the emerging hormones of a twenty year old and a desire to get out into the world. This man could help me on both counts.

I was reminded of something Granny Bill often said about West Virginia.

"Girls got three choices here in West Virginia—get pregnant, get religion, or get out!"

I was opting for number three. Number two had been appealing, and still offered comfort in the beauty of the church and the music, but the small-town hypocrisy of the Pentecostals had soured me on the notion of number two. I didn't know what to believe anymore. And I wasn't ready to consider number one.

Having maintained my first base promise to myself for twenty years, I thought I was ready for marriage and sex. I wanted a grown-up life; I wanted to move on. Royce said he'd wanted to marry me the first time he laid eyes on me. What did he see when he looked at me? I wondered. He was a talented actor, writer, and director, had a worldly veneer about him, and he, too, wanted to be rid of the constrictions and small town attitudes of his family.

I realized there was no way my mother would have rights over me if I were married.

I'd finally found the way out.

Deep down, Jack's familiarity had frightened me in some way. Too much like family, perhaps; he liked my parents and he was a West Virginia boy whom I feared had too many roots in the mountains. Truth be told, however, I didn't know how to be in a healthy, loving relationship. I was barely connected to my own self, and sharing myself would mean breaking it all up again. I couldn't go there. I was afraid he'd ask for more than I knew how to give. How could I engage in the give and take that happily married people spoke of?

I was in the throes of birthing myself; I couldn't give myself away so soon.

Was there some inherent wisdom in me, after all, that it was time—and there was opportunity—for me to come into my own, to cut the cord completely and take my chances? There were no roots, no history with Royce. He wanted a partner, one who could work alongside him or have her own work and do what she pleased—not a traditional wife.

I liked the sound of that. We could start anew, leave all the past behind, I told myself.

At some level I feared that someday I would leave Jack or he would tire of me, and I couldn't bear the familiarity of that pain; I couldn't afford to care that much. After all, my mother's DNA was in my blood. "Better to break it off now," I reasoned.

Royce was an unknown quantity, and I was betting on the long shot.

I sent Jack an awkward letter saying I was sorry, and, at the end of my junior year, eloped with the rainmaker without telling a soul. I didn't even give Jack the opportunity to talk about it. With no idea where this new relationship would take me, I told myself it would be someplace far away from the familiar turmoil—someplace where I could breathe easy and not anticipate danger around every corner, every phone call—a place where I could see clearly and leave the past behind.

I was ripe for the challenge. I'd gotten good at navigating new experiences, after all. I was used to starting over, starting with nothing, reinventing myself. I had survived without a roadmap before, and I could do it again. It seemed the only way at the time.

It was many years later before I realized I had done exactly as my mother had done at sixteen. And then some.

Epilogue

The Call That Changes Things

More than 30 years later, March 1996, Lexington, Kentucky

It's after ten when the phone rings. Seeing my mother's name on the caller ID, I listen to the fourth ring while deciding whether to answer. In my experience, late-night calls are seldom good news. And I don't usually pick up anyway, convincing myself I'll call her back the next day. Sometimes I do; sometimes I don't.

Each of our conversations begins the same way: "I haven't heard from you in a couple of months. I was getting worried. Are you okay?" Words of concern wrapped in emotional daggers meant to punish me for the thousands of ways I've failed her. That's why I'd rather be the one to initiate the call; I can do it when I feel strong enough.

She actually requires little on the phone—an *uh huh* or *no kidding* from time to time—as she drones on about life in her double-wide trailer park in Florida, complaining about the neighbor's dog disturbing her sleep with his barking or her constipation caused by all the medicines she takes. She goes on about Tom and Jerry, her aged Boston terriers—how smart they are, the tricks they perform, the food she's prepared for them that day. She'll gossip for forty-five minutes or more about people I've never met and probably never will. It's the least I can do, I remind myself each time we talk. She's an old woman now, living alone. Both my father and Granny Bill died years before and her last husband had died only a few years earlier. I need to be patient. When my urge to punish her overrides that patience, I always end up apologizing.

Tonight's call is different.

"I'm afraid I've got some bad news," she says.

I really don't want to hear this. I've had enough of her bad news over the years—the tearful alcohol-driven calls in the middle of the night, asking me what she should do about my father's drinking or about some slight from another man she's seeing. Bad news from her could be cockroaches on the kitchen counter or the death of a friend of a friend. It seldom concerns me or relates to anyone I know.

I gather up my nightgown and sit down at the kitchen table. This will be a long call. "What's happening, Mom?" I say impatiently.

"Well, I went to the doctor, and he said the cancer has come back. I thought you should know."

I close my eyes. I know where this is headed. This cancer has been reappearing in various places in her body over the last few years.

"He said he could do a second round of chemo and radiation, but he didn't think it would help me much. Besides, I don't want to go through that again."

I'm suddenly calm, asking all the questions that come to mind: Are the doctors certain? Does she want a second opinion? How is she feeling now? What does she need?

"Well, the doctor told me I had three months left, and he'd give me whatever medicine I needed for the pain . . . ."

The silence on both ends of the line smothers me. All I can say is, "I'm so sorry, Mom. I'm so sorry."

"Oh, honey, it's okay. I'm sorry to put all this on you . . . ."

She begins to cry and I wipe the tears covering my own face.

"Mother, mother, mother," I groan. "I am so sorry."

The seconds, even minutes, fly by as we share this grief with silence and tears. I've not had what you'd call a good relationship with her for years—although, strangely enough, if someone asked her, she'd say we were close. Close, because she needs to see things that way. In truth, she knows little about the ambiguities of my life. It is always about her.

Her needs. Her preferences. Her requirements. Nothing had changed. Except me. I had changed. I understood her better these days and didn't have to rely on her. I tried to be kind when I could.

"I'll be down as soon as I can get a flight," I finally tell her. "We'll figure things out together. Try not to worry."

She mumbles a thank you and we hang up.

I'm stunned by the depth of my feeling for her at this moment. I look around the kitchen—my kitchen, my home, my refuge. A place I've worked hard for, where I can be myself, where I feel safe, free of her demands and expectations and miseries. I'm proud of myself, but I'm not so safe, after all.

Folding my arms on the table, head down, I begin to cry, for her and for me, for the past and the future. Once again, a little girl, crying for her mommy.

Past hurts don't matter now. They are mere details along the road of life.

*As a river wends its way through mountains, valleys, dales, to
finally arrive at the waiting Sea, so each and every life force
dances little jigs through events and circumstances until it's
merely vapour in an occasional thought, soon too to disappear
like a river into sea.*

In Simple Terms *and* Beneath the Ordinary, Helen Howell,
author & poet

Still Not Doing It Right

April 1996, Lexington, Kentucky

The trip back to Lexington is marred only by the frequency with
which my mother asks for morphine.

Despite the considerable dosage, she remains relatively alert
and speaks charmingly, even flirtatiously, to the man in the window
seat next to her on the plane. She tells him the reason for her trip and
gives several medical details before I can distract her and mouth,
"I'm sorry," to the stranger, who seems to grasp the situation. This
same stranger helps her off the plane while I gather luggage and
look for the friend who was waiting to drive us home. The stranger
chucks a big, "Good luck!" to me as he hastens out the door of
Lexington's Bluegrass Airport. My brother and sister-in-law stayed
behind in West Palm Beach to close up my mother's place.

Once we reach my house, Mother refuses the hospital bed
I'd ordered and placed in the dining room, saying she prefers the
couch in the living room. She refuses food, saying she has no taste

left, and asks for another dose of morphine. Thus begins a routine that lasts for nearly a month. All of her heart medicine, cholesterol medicine, drugs for other symptoms and pains are discarded in favor of the liquid gold. She screams in pain as each dose starts to wear off, and, once calmed, wants to talk.

She talks about dying, how she's tried to be a good mother, how she appreciates my patience with her. It isn't a conversation; just her, talking out everything. As a result of the electroshock therapy she had in the 1960's—the year following my elopement, my leaving home—the specifics of our past history, of my life with her, are gone. She has little, if any, memory of our life before then. Our history, in her mind, begins when I am in my mid twenties. There is no way to go back.

I try hard to stay present and be rational about her monologues, acknowledging her feelings and her beliefs, even though they are far from my own. She's unafraid of dying and comforted by her belief she'll see Jesus.

At times I leave the room, just to shed my own tears, just to get a breath of life.

"Don't you worry," she tells me. "I'm going to heaven and I'll be just fine."

Her doctor advises giving her as much morphine as she asks for. Yet, I've never been in a situation like this; how much is too much? Am I overdoing it? She is always in pain without it, so I rely on the doctor's advice and that of the Hospice nurse. The nurse explains there is nothing more to do but alleviate her pain and hold her hand. There is nothing, however, that can absolve the guilt I feel that I am helping her die.

One day, with the Hospice angel sitting beside her, she screams for me to come. She'd felt a little better that morning and was sitting up in a chair, covered by blankets. I was busy making phone calls to my brother and other family members, knowing it was only a matter of days.

"My feet are going to sleep," she yells. "I need you to come rub my feet!"

I pull up a chair and begin to massage her cold feet.

"You're not doing it right, Janet!" she cries. "You're not helping."

I shake my head and hold back the tears as I attempt to massage life into the growing numbness in her feet. I remove my shoe and gently place my bare foot in her lap.

"Then, show me how," I tell her.

She closes her eyes and leans back in the chair.

Moments later, my mother is dead.

Hurricane Rains

Sixteen Years Later, 2012, Lexington, Kentucky

Hurricane-driven storms from New Orleans and Poxatawnee, Florida, break the hot spell we've endured for weeks. Everybody's praying for rain, alarmed at the deep cracks in the soil, the grit, the dried yellow leaves on tomato plants, the lethargy nurtured by the blistering heat.

With little warning, the rains come. Heavy, beating and blowing rain, thunder and lightning as if the sky would break in pieces, as if it were having a nervous breakdown. In an instant, everything that had been parched and dry is saturated. Burned, seedy lawns gulp water like prickly pears in the desert. Porch pillows, dusted with layers of pollen, airborne dirt and cement powder from recent street repairs, slump into smiling, soggy bags. The braided welcome rug expands with wet relief. Everything adjusts its point of gravity to locate somewhere other than where it had been during the months-long drought.

Inside the house, I open doors and windows, freeing the smell of the dog, the sweat of old laundry undone, the heaviness of left-over frying oil on the back burner of the stove.

The wetness changes everything. Labels slide off beer bottles. Pieces of table puzzles swell and lose their place. Post-ems on refrigerators drift off, with little trace of where they've been. The rooms exhale a heavy, stale breath and draw in new life.

I stand on the front porch, welcoming the rain, my face misted and cooled, my body baptized with each drop.

"It's time," I shudder, turning my face up to the rumbling sky.

"I can bury her ashes now."

Discussion

1. What characterizes a willful person?
2. Which character does *A Willful Child* most effectively describe? How?
3. Can you relate to the women in this book? In what way(s)?
4. Moving from one place to another is difficult for the child. What, if anything, does she learn from these experiences?
5. How would you describe Janet's mother? Her father? Her Granny Bill?
6. How would you describe the child's relationship with her mother?
7. The child is often caught in a double-bind with her parents, where she can't win. Have you ever been in a similar situation? How did it make you feel? How did you handle it? Was your behavior effective?
8. The child unwillingly becomes a keeper of her mother's secrets. How do secrets affect this relationship?
9. The author mentions suicide twice in the book. Why does she see this as an alternative?
10. What does the author mean when she refers to "me/not me?"
11. Can you imagine yourself in the child's circumstances? How would you behave?
12. The young woman speaks of "getting above her raising." What is she talking about here? Why does it hurt so much when her mother accuses her of "getting above her raising?" Can you relate to this? Are there things your mother or father have said to you when you were young that "cut deep?"
13. Where are the "turning points" in this child's life? How are they positive? Negative?
14. What do you think of the teenager's decision to break with Jack? Was her reasoning sound? Why? Why not?
15. The narrator of the story shifts perspective at times, between a child's eye view and that of an adult looking back at her past. How effective is the author in separating these two points of view?
16. The young woman finally sees what she considers *a way out.* What do you think of her decision? Can you think of another way she might have handled it?

The author welcomes your thoughts on the book.
She can be reached at awillfulchild@gmail.com

Photographs

About the Author

A graduate of Marshall University and SUNY-Stony Brook, Janet Steele Holloway left Appalachia to live in NYC for twenty-five years, then returned to the region in 1990. She is the founder of Women Leading Kentucky, Inc., a successful non-profit designed to create opportunities for women to lead, learn and give back to their communities. Janet has managed statewide small business programs for New Jersey and Kentucky and served as president of the national Association of Small Business Development Centers in 1993. She has published profiles of business leaders in various media including *Entrepreneur Magazine* and *Business Lexington.* She was recognized as a finalist in the Best Writers Competition in 2008, and again in 2011, in the Harriet Rose Legacy Competition, both sponsored by the Carnegie Center for Literacy & Learning. As a child, Janet set a goal of visiting all 48 states and reached this goal but still has North Dakota and Alaska on her list since there are now 50. She plans to travel to Alaska in the spring of 2013. This Logan County, West Virginia native lives in Lexington, KY, loves to travel and continues to write.

Made in the USA
Lexington, KY
08 May 2014